T0343374

aud Risk Management
Practical guide for accountants

AMSTERDAM • BOSTON • HEIDELBERG • LONDON
NEW YORK • OXFORD • PARIS • SAN DIEGO
SAN FRANCISCO • SINGAPORE • SYDNEY • TOKYO

CIMA Publishing is an imprint of Elsevier

CIMA

PUBLISHING

VIER

CIMA Publishing is an imprint of Elsevier
Linacre House, Jordan Hill, Oxford OX2 8DP, UK
30 Corporate Drive, Suite 400, Burlington, MA 01803, USA

First edition 2008

Copyright © 2008 Elsevier Ltd. All rights reserved

No part of this publication may be reproduced, stored in a retrieval system
or transmitted in any form or by any means electronic, mechanical, photocopying,
recording or otherwise without the prior written permission of the publisher

Permissions may be sought directly from Elsevier's Science & Technology Rights
Department in Oxford, UK: phone (+44) (0) 1865 843830; fax (+44) (0) 1865 853333;
e-mail: permissions@elsevier.com. Alternatively you can submit your request online
by visiting the Elsevier web site at http://elsevier.com/locate/permissions, and
selecting *Obtaining permission to use Elsevier material*

Notice
No responsibility is assumed by the publisher for any injury and/or damage to persons
or property as a matter of products liability, negligence or otherwise, or from any use
or operation of any methods, products, instructions or ideas contained in the material
herein.

British Library Cataloguing in Publication Data
A catalogue record for this book is available from the British Library

978 0 7506 8381 4

For information on all CIMA publications
visit our website at books.elsevier.com

Typeset by Integra Software Services Pvt. Ltd, Pondicherry, India
www.integra-india.com

Printed and bound in Great Britain

08 09 10 11   10 9 8 7 6 5 4 3 2 1

Working together to grow
libraries in developing countries

www.elsevier.com | www.bookaid.org | www.sabre.org

ELSEVIER   BOOK AID   Sabre Foundation
              International

Contents

Section 1: Fraud – Typologies and Trends   **1**

1   Legal Definitions of, and the Law Relating to, Fraud   **3**

1.1	What is fraud?	5
1.2	The hallmarks of a fraud	7
1.3	Estimates of fraud volumes, and trends identified	8
1.4	The law relating to fraud	13
1.5	Case law	20
1.6	Overseas law and UK companies	23
1.7	Non-Statutory codes and guidance on fraud risk management	24
1.8	Conclusion	24

2   Different Types of Fraud   **25**

2.1	General	27
2.2	General introduction to fraud typologies	27
2.3	Some examples of specific frauds	29
2.4	What types of fraud is your business most vulnerable to?	34

3   Analytical Methods in Fraud Risk Management   **37**

3.1	Planning	39
3.2	Gathering information about the business	39
3.3	Fraud risk factors	41
3.4	Assessing the risks, taking account of internal controls	43
3.5	Involving the management team	44
3.6	Responding to identified fraud indicators/fraud risks	45
3.7	Fraud indicators	46
3.8	Statistical/technological tools in fraud risk analysis	48
3.9	Cultural issues in fraud risk management	48

Section 2: Risks, and the Systems to Counter Them   **51**

4   Internal Frauds   **53**

4.1	Vulnerability to internal frauds	55
4.2	Some typical internal frauds	57

5 External Frauds 65

5.1	Introduction	67
5.2	Supplier frauds	67
5.3	Customer frauds	68
5.4	Embezzlement	70
5.5	Investment fraud	70
5.6	Third party-against-customer fraud	72
5.7	If disaster strikes	73

6 Information, Network and Internet Security – What the Non-IT Professional Needs to Know 75

6.1	Assessing the environment – questions your IT expert may ask	77
6.2	Securing the technology in a fraud investigation	78
6.3	Capturing the electronic evidence	80
6.4	Examining the images taken	81
6.5	What sorts of information may be recovered? – historic records	82
6.6	What sort of information may be recovered? – ongoing monitoring	83

Section 3: Post-event Fraud Management – What to Do When Your Concerns Are Aroused That a Fraud Has Taken Place or Is Being Attempted 85

7 The Immediate Steps 87

7.1	Receipt of a fraud suspicion report	89
7.2	Common first steps	91
7.3	Securing the evidence	91
7.4	Assembling the investigation team	95
7.5	Overseeing external communications	97
7.6	Legal issues on an investigation	98
7.7	Preserving, tracing and recovering lost assets	99

8 Investigation Techniques and Next Steps 101

8.1	Interviewing witnesses	103
8.2	How to carry on the interview	104
8.3	Separate representation	105
8.4	Considering employment issues	106
8.5	Post-investigation de-briefing	107
8.6	Securing the assets	108
8.7	Prevention of further fraud	109
8.8	Directors' duties and solvency	109
8.9	Recovery of funds	111

9 Dealing with External Parties: Regulators, Insurers and the Law Enforcement Authorities   **115**

9.1	General	117
9.2	Dealing with regulators	117
9.3	Dealing with the Police/other Law Enforcement Authorities	121
9.4	Dealing with the company's bankers	122
9.5	Dealing with the company's insurers	123
9.6	Dealing with the stock market (listed companies)	123

10 The Aftermath of a Fraud: Reputational Issues   **125**

10.1	General	127
10.2	Internal communications	128
10.3	Questions to consider in the event of a fraud risk crisis	129
10.4	Public relations	131

11 Some Aspects of The Law re Evidence, Privilege and Fraud Investigation   **133**

11.1	Legal issues on an investigation	135
11.2	The concept of privilege	135
11.3	Privilege and investigation reports	136
11.4	Maintaining privilege	137
11.5	Case law: *Director of the Serious Fraud Office ex parte Smith*	139
11.6	Fraud investigations and the requirement to disclose	142
11.7	What types of document should you be most concerned about?	147
11.8	Document management to preserve privilege	152
11.9	Document retention	153
11.10	Law regathering evidence	155

Index   **159**

Section 1

Fraud – Typologies and Trends

Legal Definitions of, and the Law Relating to, Fraud

1.1   What is fraud?

Until recently, there was no precise legal definition in English law of "fraud" (there was, however, an offence of *conspiracy to defraud*, and consequently a definition of this – but as conspiracy requires the collusion of more than one person, those deceptions carried out by one person alone were not included).

> *Note:* Scotland, for the record, does and has for some time had a common law crime of fraud; this is considered to arise when someone achieves a practical outcome through a false pretence.

Many commentators felt this was a considerable weakness in the English legal system. Their view was that a definition flexible enough to capture a wider range of frauds would allow for the prosecution of many "cons" which otherwise wriggled through the net, for want of an offence which clearly fit them neatly.

This is because fraudsters, in the absence of a specific offence of fraud, generally had to be prosecuted under one or more of eight offences created under the Thefts Acts 1968–96. These offences were, essentially, the carrying out of the following acts *dishonestly and with deception*:

- Obtaining property belonging to another;
- Obtaining a money transfer;
- Obtaining services;
- Securing the remission of an existing liability to make a payment;
- Inducing a creditor to wait for payment, or to forego payment, with intent to permanently default on the debt to that creditor;
- Obtaining an exemption from, or abatement of, a liability to make a payment;
- Obtaining a pecuniary advantage; or
- Procuring the execution of a valuable security.

Some frauds, however, were hard to make fit neatly into the definitions of these offences – and often, a prosecution would cite many of the above, so as to give them the best possible chance of a conviction. Nonetheless there were still a variety of loopholes, and the situation was far from satisfactory.

In addition, the Government itself pointed out that the existing legislation was in some areas inappropriate for dealing with 21st-century frauds – that is, they did not always cope well with deceptions facilitated using new technologies.

To meet this perceived weakness, the Fraud Act 2006 has been enacted and came into force on 15 January 2007. Among other things, it defines a new offence of fraud, which would be fulfilled by any of the following three conditions:

1. *Fraud by false representation* – that is, when someone pretends to be someone other than who they really are, or to be doing something they are not, or selling something they don't possess;
2. *Fraud by failing to disclose information* – that is, keeping quiet about the true facts of a situation. This form of the offence has sparked some legal debate, since it seems to go further than the existing case law (for example Derry v. Peek [1889] generally taken as authoritative on the issue of misleading);
3. *Fraud by abuse of position* – that is, someone taking advantage of their special position. The issue of what positions might be covered by the Act is not defined, although it seems likely that fiduciary positions (positions of trust) would be caught.

The newly-established offence of fraud carries a maximum penalty of 10 years' imprisonment.

In an announcement, a representative of the Home Office said: "The Act replaces the existing complicated array of over-specific and overlapping deception offences. These offences have proved inadequate to tackle the wide range of possible fraudulent activity today or keep pace with rapidly developing technology."

On the same subject, the Home Office Minister Gerry Sutcliffe said: "The new Fraud Act will make an important contribution to the fight against fraud. It will remove the deficiencies in the existing provisions and establish an effective criminal law that is flexible enough to capture the true breadth of fraud today."

Source: Home Office Statement (http://www.homeoffice.gov.uk/about-us/news/crime-bills).

The new Act has therefore been drafted with an eye to closing many of the loopholes opened by the advance of technology. For example, it outlaws the writing and possession of software or data, knowing that it is designed – or adapted – for fraudulent purposes.

This should help close the door on such email scams as "phishing" – the sending of large numbers of emails, in bulk, which attempt to lure the recipient into disclosing their bank account or credit card details.

Under the new Act, the simple possession of computer files or software, prepared for use in a phishing expedition, is criminalised (whether or not the phishing actually takes place).

Note: As we have already seen, although there was no definition of fraud when carried out by a single perpetrator, there *was* a common-law offence of *conspiracy to defraud* – the limitation of which was the requirement for more than one person to be involved. It was proposed that this offence should be repealed with the introduction of the Fraud Act 2006, since the activity would be covered by the more general definition of fraud. However, it was felt wise to leave it on the statute books until the new legislation has been tried and tested – so the offence of conspiracy to defraud still exists.

Setting aside the legal definitions, in common language fraud is usually taken to include a range of forms of deception, carried out with the intention of gain for oneself (or harm to another). It may include a range of activities – some of which are themselves defined criminal offences – such as:

- Forgery
- Deception
- Misrepresentation (but as we will see in Section 1.2 below, accidental misrepresentation would not normally be caught)
- Collusion
- Misappropriation
- In many cases, theft.

1.2 The hallmarks of a fraud

So is it possible for us to step outside the legalese for a moment, and identify some common factors which should alert us to the fact that what we are looking at is probably a fraud?

The answer is "yes": commentators typically describe a fraud as being characterised by the following three elements:

1. *Deception.* Someone (usually but not always, or not only, the victim of the
   fraud) must have been misled in some way.
2. *Dishonesty and intent.* This misleading must generally have been dishonest
   and intentional, not accidental. However care should be exercised if, for
   example, a misrepresentation was made in a negligent or cavalier manner.
3. *Materiality of that deception.* The deception must have led to someone's
   detriment or loss. A non-material misrepresentation, whether intentional or
   not, which causes no loss or detriment, would not usually be deemed to be
   fraudulent.

1.3 Estimates of fraud volumes, and trends identified

Volumes of fraud are hard to quantify – not least because concrete numbers are
available only on those cases which are actually reported and end up in the courts
(and even then these are not easily identified and collated).

Of course, a large number of cases which *are* discovered are never reported, often
because businesses are unwilling to incur the reputational damage that might arise
from a discussion of the flaws in their systems and controls. On top of this, it is
impossible to guess at the number of frauds which are never discovered at all –
the perpetrators getting away with the proceeds of their activities.

What *can* be said with some confidence is that – despite efforts to combat fraud –
the volumes and numbers are rising. For example:

- Figures from a survey conducted by KPMG Forensic (KPMG Fraud Barome-
  ter, July 2002) indicated that from 1 January 2002 to 30 June 2002 fraud cases
  in the UK went up by over 150 per cent compared with the same period in
  the previous year, and totalled some £255m. The surge in volume was in part
  attributable to a large increase in frauds in the banking and finance sector;
  rising public sector fraud (e.g. tax and VAT evasion) also contributed.
- Moving on by 3 years, the same survey indicated yet further rises in the
  levels of fraud in the UK – in 2005, they hit £900m (and again, as we have
  mentioned, this report only captured those frauds of over £100,000 which
  went to court).
- In the first 6 months of 2006, the survey estimated UK frauds at some £650m
  as compared to £249m in the first 6 months of 2005.

t all points to an inexorable rise. Other estimates, based on different metrics, nevertheless give a similar and alarming picture. For example, APACS, the UK trade association for payments services providers, estimated that credit card fraud fell in the first 6 months of 2005 from £229m to £209m; but it also estimated that online banking fraud had *increased* from £14m to £22m, in the same period: an indication, perhaps, that where businesses make progress in preventing fraud in one area, the fraudsters will quickly turn their attention to locating the next vulnerable point in the system.

Of course, it is likely that at least some of this increase is attributable not just to rising levels of fraud itself – but to more rigorous requirements in terms of regulatory reporting and disclosure, particularly in the regulated sectors such as banking and financial services. In fact it is often these regulated businesses, with their mandatory fraud reporting infrastructures, which are the most likely to identify, report and prosecute frauds – those which do not have to, may well prefer to keep a low profile, and lick their wounds in private.

Recovery rates are also typically highest in these industries, perhaps because if they are compelled to identify and report them – and are therefore dragged into the spotlight whether they like it or not – they then have an interest in being seen to do all they can to protect their shareholders' and customers' interests by bringing the perpetrators to book.

Nonetheless, recovery rates are not typically high: again, evidence is patchy – in part because recoveries are themselves not formally reported on. Further, actual recoveries may differ significantly from any court awards – some recoveries may be made from perpetrators in return for an agreement not to prosecute; others may be mandated by the courts, but never actually made because the perpetrator no longer has the funds.

In some cases a defrauded business' insurers may also provide a measure of protection – but many businesses are still woefully under-insured, perhaps because their owners and managers are unaware of, or unconvinced by, the benefits of employee fidelity policies and the like. Others may choose not to claim on their policies where the amounts are small, or where the recovery may be outweighed by the impact on their premium.

And are we learning from our experiences? Well, possibly... but then again, possibly not. A further survey – this time published by Ernst & Young's Fraud Investigation Group in May 2000 ("Fraud, The Unmanaged Risk", an international survey of the effect of fraud on business, co-ordinated by Ernst & Young Fraud

Investigation Group) – suggested that not only were many companies failing to get to grips adequately with the theoretically present risks of fraud – but they were also failing to learn from past mistakes, even when they discovered that they had already fallen victim to a fraud!

Who is doing all this defrauding?

Sadly, it is mainly your beloved colleagues! Some 80 per cent odd of serious frauds against businesses are estimated to be carried out by staff – whether acting alone, or colluding with an external third party. And although hard numbers are – yet again – hard to come by, it also seems that a relatively high proportion are carried out by the more senior staff. This is despite the fact that they are likely to be on higher salaries, and therefore – arguably – under less personal financial pressures than their more junior colleagues. It seems most probable that it is because of the greater opportunity they have, both in terms of avoiding controls to carry out the fraud, and in terms of covering their tracks.

Longevity seems no guarantee of loyalty to a company, either; it is not just senior managers who seem to be more prone to defrauding their employers – a disproportionate amount seem to be carried out by people who have been with the business for some time (that is to say, 5 years or more). This implies that whilst recruitment policies are important in minimising the risk of employee fraud, so are proper review procedures for the activities of existing staff – including senior staff.

Increasing incidence of computer-related fraud

No-one engaged in business can be oblivious to its increasing reliance on computers, or to the rising volumes of business conducted over the internet. These changes bring with them many benefits – speed, economy and some aspects of disintermediation among them; but they also foster new risks and challenges, not least from the perspective of fraud prevention. Thus it is unsurprising that computer fraud is one of the fastest-rising concerns of fraud risk managers.

These risks include:

- The unauthorised electronic transfer of funds or other assets;
- Manipulation of programs or computer records to disguise the details of a transaction;
- Hacking into an organisation's systems in order to manipulate, or steal, data over the internet or otherwise.

For many, however, computer crime is particularly challenging because it is regarded as somewhat "mysterious" to non-IT professionals; and many risk managers harbour a lurking anxiety that their risk mitigation processes could be improved.

Preventative measures

In terms of remedial action, organisations' processes seem to vary very much with the size of the organisation (or in some cases, size and nature of parentage – since group policies and procedures may be applied to subsidiaries of the group no matter what their individual scale).

A number of surveys have linked the size of an organisation (typically measured by reference to its turnover) to the likelihood of its having established a formal fraud risk management policy and fraud reporting procedures, and of its taking such steps as fraud awareness training and the use of a fraud hotline.

The second most powerful factor is the organisation's regulated status, since regulators in certain industries place a requirement on their licence-holders to have in place, and report on the efficiency of, their anti-fraud measures.

The most obvious example of this is the financial services industry, where the UK's regulator – the Financial Services Authority – places clear obligations not only on authorised businesses but on their senior personnel to have in place appropriate systems and controls for the mitigation of risks.

Less frequently, a strong set of fraud-prevention processes may be brought about by specific fraud events (those firms with a weak culture of fraud avoidance also seemingly being poor at learning from experience!), or – for larger firms – a specific review of the organisation's vulnerabilities in this area. Such a review is often initiated at the request of the organisation's audit committee or internal audit department; this fact alone implies that this will be the case only with larger or more highly regulated organisations, since smaller and more entrepreneurial ones are less likely even to have established such committees/functions.

Although we will look in more depth at specific anti-fraud measures later in this book, it is worth noting at this point some of the most basic, but powerful, measures that firms are employing. They include:

- Establishing an organisation-wide regime of documented and considered internal controls;
- Periodic fraud-awareness training for staff;
- The fostering of an anti-fraud culture;

- Well-publicised protection for whistleblowers and the identification of a senior member of staff to whom staff can report their suspicions (in some cases on an anonymous basis);
- Mandatory staff holidays of sufficient duration (typically 2 weeks) which can allow many issues to emerge;
- Ensuring that there is a periodic review of such controls, in terms both of their continued efficacy and of adherence to them;
- Password security for IT systems.

Governments' reaction to the rising tide of fraud

Shortly, we are going to look at some of the laws which applies in the context of fraud. You'll note that there have been various updates to, and increases in, legislation and regulation in this area, despite the fact that fraud itself is nothing new.

What *is* new, perhaps, is the backdrop against which these events occur – some of them very high profile (Enron, Worldcom, Parmalat) and some of them less so.

Firstly, there is rising public disquiet at the perception of wrongdoing, sometimes at the highest level, within large and often publicly listed companies; a sense that the people to whom individuals entrust their money – whether as investors in a company, or as its customers – should be held properly accountable for what they do and how they spend that money.

But secondly, fraudulent activity is often believed to be associated with terrorist funding, an issue high on the agenda of many governments. Politicians and law-makers are keen to be seen to act swiftly and firmly to protect their people, with a view to both to protecting their local economies and to maintaining investor confidence – something which was badly shaken in the months following September 11, 2001, for example.

This is something of a sea change: governments have not always been so ready to intervene. In past decades, many were happy to leave it to the markets to absorb the effects of large-scale fraud. Now, however, that approach is not seen as nearly robust enough – and governments are taking a much harder line ("tough on crime, tough on the causes of crime"). They are granting, and regulatory bodies and law enforcement agencies are using, a wide range of enforcement and information-gathering powers – and there is more talk than ever before on subjects such as "corporate governance". In effect, the officers and senior employees of companies are now subject to much greater responsibility, liability and accountability for the activities of the organisations they work for.

1.4 The law relating to fraud

In this section we will consider the various UK statutes which relate to fraud – whether in dealing with fraud offences, or in other regards (e.g. disclosure, reporting requirements and the like).

The Fraud Act 2006

We have already looked at this act in brief, earlier in this Chapter. In summary, the new act, which came into force on 15 January 2007, created a general offence of fraud – with a maximum penalty of ten years in prison, and/or a fine – which can be committed in any one of three ways:

1. False representation (including implied misrepresentations).
2. Failing to disclose information.
3. Abusing a position.

This general offence of fraud focuses on the perpetrator's *intentions* (i.e. as opposed to the actual outcome of what he has done, for example whether someone has been deceived). It is likely that this may lead to it being used in preference to other offences, under other laws, since those may focus on outcomes (e.g. current market abuse and insider dealing legislation).

The new Act also creates some new offences, for example:

- of obtaining services dishonestly; and
- of possessing, making and supplying articles for use in frauds.

In addition, it covers some activities involving newer technologies. For example:

- It updates the definition of an "account", as it was defined under Section 24A of the Theft Act 1968. (This made it an offence for a person to retain a credit made to his account, knowing or believing that the credit was derived from fraud, theft, blackmail or stolen goods). The new definition now includes electronic money accounts, as well as conventional bank accounts.
- It covers the creation or possession of software which has been created or adapted for use in fraud.

In terms of territorial scope, the new Act also gives the UK courts jurisdiction in cases where the **only** element of activity to have taken place in the UK is the gain or loss of property. This may enable prosecutions to be brought which hitherto could not – because the relevant activities had gone on elsewhere.

The Enterprise Act 2002

This received Royal Assent on 7 November 2002, and has since come into effect in tranches. It incorporates a number of provisions aimed at dealing with corporate fraud – essentially, these are aimed at building on other provisions made in the Competition Act 1998, which was itself directed at preventing cartels.

However, in contrast with the Competition Act (whose provisions apply to the companies themselves), the relevant provisions of the Enterprise Act bite on individuals.

These relatively new offences carry a maximum prison sentence of five years. They centre on an individual's "dishonesty" and address such cartel-oriented and anti-competitive issues as:

- price-fixing;
- market-sharing;
- the limitation of production; and
- bid-rigging.

The Proceeds of Crime Act 2002

This received Royal Assent in July 2002. Whilst on the face of it this act deals with money laundering (i.e. activities including the disguising of the criminal origins of money), you should remember that at some point the funds or other assets which have been defrauded from a business, or its shareholders, customers, counterparties or employees, will themselves become the proceeds of crime. Thus, this act may well be one under which a valid prosecution could be brought – and given the wide information-gathering and confiscation powers granted to the law enforcement agencies under it, it may be their preferred choice.

The act achieved a number of aims, which we will review briefly, including:

- an extension of the range of money laundering offences which had previously been defined;
- the introduction of various reporting requirements relating to money laundering;
- The establishment of the Assets Recovery Agency (ARA).

Taking these in order:

- *Money laundering.* Under the act, someone commits a money laundering offence if he conceals, disguises, converts or transfers criminal property or removes it from England, Wales, Scotland or Northern Ireland.
- He may also commit an offence if he enters into or becomes concerned in an arrangement that he knows or suspects facilitates (by whatever means) the acquisition, retention, use or control of criminal property by or on behalf of another person, or if he acquires, uses or has possession of criminal property.
- From this it will be apparent that many activities aimed at defrauding a business (or its staff, counterparties or customers), or assisting in such activities (however peripherally), may also be money laundering offences.
- The act extended the range of money laundering offences to cover the proceeds of *any* criminal conduct, not just – as had previously been the case – "serious" crime. That is, there is no *de minimis* limit – and further, no need for the offensive conduct to have been carried on in, or have any connection with, the UK.
- Further, the act does not distinguish, in the offence of acquisition, use and possession of the proceeds of crime, between the original criminal and a later recipient of the proceeds of a crime: so a later recipient may be as culpable as the original launderer.
- *Reporting requirements.* Prior to the introduction of this act, there were several offences of failure to make a "Suspicious Transaction Report", or similar, under laws such as the Drug Trafficking Act 1994 and the Money Laundering Regulations 1993. The act has broadened the scope of these offences, and brought the various offences closer in line with one another, by creating three new offences of failure to disclose. Effectively:
  - People working in the "regulated sector" (a term which is defined in a schedule to the act, but which typically means financial services businesses), who come by information in the course of their business that should give them reasonable grounds to suspect money laundering, commit an offence if they fail to make a report to their business' "Money Laundering Reporting Officer (MLRO)".
  - Following on from this, MLROs in the regulated sector commit an offence if one of their colleagues makes a report to them that gives *them* reasonable grounds for suspicion, and they do not themselves then make an onward suspicious-transaction report to the appropriate law enforcement authority.

- The MLROs outside the regulated sector commit an offence if they do not make a suspicion report when they know or suspect, as a result of a disclosure made to them, that someone is engaged in money laundering (this is slightly less onerous than the obligation on finance sector MLROs, who may fall foul if there are reasonable grounds for suspicion – even if they were not actually suspicious).
- Because there is no *de minimis* limit, the reporting obligations apply even in respect of very small cases of potential laundering. This has undoubtedly sparked a number of defensive reports on the part of finance sector firms – including in the case of some frauds.
- *The Assets Recovery Agency* established under the act carries out investigations with a view to confiscating the proceeds of crime, recovering those proceeds through civil proceedings, and the taxing of criminal proceeds.

The Public Interest Disclosure Act 1988 (PIDA)

This act was introduced in the wake of a number of corporate financial scandals, including the collapse, as a result of a several $bn fraud, of the Bank of Credit and Commerce International ("BCCI") – see box below.

Case study: The Bank of Credit and Commerce International (BCCI)

The collapse of BCCI was triggered when on 5 July 1991, the regulatory authorities of 7 different countries (the Cayman Islands, France, Luxembourg, Spain, Switzerland, the UK and the US) simultaneously raided the offices of its branches.

The raid and consequent seizure of control of the bank, brought to an end some two decades of mounting mismanagement which included fraudulent record keeping, bad lending, breach of bank ownership regulations and money laundering.

Whilst some of BCCI's officials actively sought to take advantage of the bank's *lack of proper governance, controls and risk management systems* in order to facilitate a variety of improper activities, others were simply *too incompetent to realise what was happening.* Above all, there was *no culture of accountability and individuals were not encouraged to raise their concerns or challenge their seniors.*

Regulators or at least some of them – had in fact been alive to the fact that dubious practices were afoot in the bank: and indeed sought to form a "college" of their number to co-ordinate supervision of the group across borders, and attempt to obtain some sort of overview of the complex and opaque structuring of the organisation. These efforts came too late, and were insufficiently decisive, however:

The lessons to be learned from this event? Among others:

- The fact that those senior executives and controllers of businesses who have, and exert, power over the firm should be controlled – or at least properly supervised, monitored and governed – by an appropriate governance framework and set of protocols;
- In the case of regulated institutions, that there is a need for clear lines of communication and information exchange, and co-ordinated supervision of multinational and complex groups;
- That training, and an environment where employees understand that they are expected to report concerns (and know how to do so, and to whom) is critical to the effectiveness of controls, where they do exist; and
- That those at the top of an organisation play a key role in setting the cultural and ethical climate of the business.

PIDA's aim was to provide a measure of protection for employees of businesses who reported their suspicions of fraudulent behaviour, on the part of their colleagues or bosses (otherwise known as "whistleblowing"). Many employees who formed such suspicions were unwilling to make the appropriate disclosures, because of their fears of reprisals; for example, an enquiry into the aforementioned BCCI collapse – the Bingham Report – revealed that whilst many employees of the bank were aware that all was not as it should have been, many were afraid to raise their concerns because of what the report termed an "autocratic environment".

The ultimate goal, therefore, was to encourage more widespread whistleblowing, and therefore better protection for businesses, their owners and their customers.

There is good evidence that this aim is being achieved: various cases support this view. An example of the type of protection – or at least remedy – provided to whistleblowers (albeit not, in this case, relating to fraud), is set out below:

Case study: *Bladon v. ALM Medical Services ET, 25 April 2000*

The Bladon case resulted in the first appeal made to the Court of Appeal, on the construction and application of the "Protected Disclosure" provisions which were inserted into Part IVA of the Employment Rights Act 1996 by PIDA.

The case related to a Mr Bladon, a registered nurse who had been employed by ALM Medical Services Limited in its nursing home business from June–September 1999. Mr Bladon began as a charge nurse at Lowther View Nursing Home, one of a number of ALM homes. During August and September he acted as matron of Lowther View, covering for sick leave. During this time he made a disclosure by telephone to the personal assistant of Dr Matta, the MD of ALM, expressing concern about patient care and welfare. Being asked to put these in writing, he did so. He then also telephoned the relevant Local Authority, and in due course spoke to Mrs Woan of the Nursing Home Inspectorate, which carried out an investigation at Lowther View in September 1999.

Following these events, Mrs Woan wrote to ALM on 8 September; Mr Bladon was given a disciplinary hearing by Dr Matta on 9 September; and he was given a written warning on 10 September. He was then summarily dismissed on 16 September 1999. He went to tribunal on 20 September 1999, alleged "Unfair Dismissal (Protected Disclosure)" and was represented by the employment union UNISON.

ALM alleged that Mr Bladon had been dismissed for reasons which "had nothing whatsoever to do with his allegations to the Nursing Inspectorate"; instead, it said, they related to serious breaches of contract committed by him, relating to the proper discipline of a male care assistant in failing to investigate an incident of possible non-accidental injury to a resident.

It also alleged that there were shortcomings in his professional attitude to staff, which it said fell well below acceptable standards and that, while on leave from ALM, he was supplied to ALM, without its management's knowledge, as an agency nurse at another of its homes. While there he had acted in bad faith, making statements to staff to the effect that he intended "to close the Mattas down for good" and asking them for "information and written statements citing any failings at Arundel Lodge for him to use as extra ammunition for his case against ALM."

The tribunal decided, unanimously, that Mr Bladon had indeed been subject to a "detriment" (a term provided for under the Employment Rights Act, as amended by PIDA) when he was given the written warning for having made a protected disclosure to the Nursing Inspectorate.

It decided that he had also been unfairly dismissed, due mainly to his having made protected disclosures to ALM and the Nursing Inspectorate. They related to danger to the health or safety of a patient, to failure or likely failure to comply with a legal obligation and possibly to the potential commission of a criminal offence; they were made in good faith and in the reasonable belief that they were true, with the aim of bringing about an investigation, which took place and substantiated most of them; and that Mr Bladon had acted reasonably in contacting Social Services nine days after his fax to Mr Matta's assistant.

The tribunal noted that on Mr Bladon's dismissal, there was no disciplinary hearing and no notice to him of the allegations against him, so that he had no opportunity to deal with the evidence. It concluded that the protected disclosures were Mr Matta's main reason for dismissing Mr Bladon. Mr Bladon was consequently awarded compensation for his unfair dismissal and the detriment to which he had been subject.

An organisation called Public Concern at Work (http://www.pcaw.co.uk/) was influential in rallying support for the introduction of PIDA. It is still in existence, and can be a helpful resource – providing:

- Confidential legal advice to employees who wish to raise concerns; and
- Employer training on good governance standards, and on how to implement effective whistleblowing policies.

The Criminal Justice Act 1987

Under this act, the Director of the Serious Fraud Office (SFO) (see Chapter 11 for more on this agency) is granted powers to require a person to answer questions, provide information, or produce documents to assist in any SFO investigation.

He is also empowered to investigate any suspected offence which appears to him to include serious or complex fraud (Section 1(3) of that act). For the definition of a "serious or complex fraud", see Chapter 11.

1.5 Case law

Case law on assisting in a fraud (Albeit with limited knowledge or understanding)

Since we have spent a little time considering the law on whistleblowing, and the situation of someone who becomes aware that a fraud as being perpetrated by someone else, we will also spend a few moments considering this question. Can a person, with a relatively limited understanding of the technicalities of a fraudulent scheme, nevertheless be found liable to those who are defrauded, even if he is not himself the "driving force" behind that fraud?

The answer is a resounding "yes", as a case reviewed by the Privy Council in 2005 showed. It held that an individual can know (and can of course suspect), that he is assisting in a fraudulent misappropriation of money – without his necessarily knowing that the money in question is held on trust for someone else (its true owner), or indeed knowing what a "trust" means at all.

In effect, the Council determined that someone who knowingly assists in a dishonest and fraudulent scheme, carried out by trustees (i.e. by people holding money for the benefit of others) to misapply that money, can be made *personally* liable to account for it alongside those trustees. Liability for such dishonest assistance requires, however, a "dishonest state of mind" on the part of the person who assists in a breach of trust.

It is worth understanding a few facts of the case, if only to ensure that you do not inadvertently allow yourself or your staff to fall foul of the law through sheer passivity!

Case Study: *Barlow Clowes International Ltd (In Liquidation)*

"C" operated a fraudulent investment scheme. Under this scheme, a company, "BC" received money which it held on trust for investors who were its clients. Most of this money was in fact dissipated on C's expensive lifestyle, and on other business ventures – whether his own, or those of an associate, "CR".

Some of the money was paid away to facilitate these activities, through bank accounts administered by an offshore financial services company of which an individual, "H", was a director.

The investment scheme eventually collapsed. The liquidator of BC claimed (*inter alia*) that H was liable for dishonestly assisting BC in the misappropriation of investors' funds.

H argued in his own defence, that there was nothing to prove that he had known anything of the contractual arrangements relating to the investors and their money – nor of the mechanisms for managing their funds. Thus, he could not have known about the dishonest misappropriation by BC.

Outcome: The Privy Council held that someone can know, and can certainly suspect, that he is assisting in a misappropriation of money without knowing that it is being held "on trust" – or indeed what a trust means.

It also decided that it was unnecessary for H to know the "precise involvement" of CR in BC's affairs, in order for him to suspect that neither CR nor anyone else had the right to use BC's money for speculative investments of their own.

Having considered the risks of what might be termed an enhanced form of wilful blindness, we will look further, but again briefly, at the issue of when one might be deemed to have knowledge of the perpetration of a fraud. Remember, however, that these are complex areas – if you are in any doubt at all, you should take appropriate legal advice: do not simply hope that any uncomfortable suspicions you may have will go away, or prove unfounded!

Case law on constructive knowledge

A couple of cases which arose in the early 1990s were helpful in clarifying when a party could be found to have "constructive knowledge" of fraudulent activity (and therefore, potentially, to have been co-operating in that fraudulent activity).

"Constructive knowledge": A concept in law which someone can be deemed to have, or to be able to infer, knowledge from the facts available.

It may also be used in the context of companies, where an organisation may be deemed to have actual knowledge even though this knowledge is based on the sum of elements of knowledge held by different individuals.

In *Agip (Africa) Limited v. Jackson & Ors CA* 21 December 1990 (*The Times*, 9 January 1991), the High Court reviewed the case of a firm of accountants, who – whilst knowing nothing of their client's fraud, were deemed in law to be "knowingly assisting" in the furtherance of a fraudulent breach of trust by helping him to conceal money in suspicious circumstances. They were thus held to be liable for sums claimed by the client's employer.

In considering the case, the Court stated that the accountants had not made the type of enquiries which honest men would have made to satisfy themselves that they were not helping to conceal or launder money.

In *Eagle Trust Plc v. SBC Securities Limited* (*Financial Times*, 5 February 1991), a firm of stockmarket underwriters had discharged their sub-underwriters' liabilities with funds that had been misappropriated by a client's chief executive.

In the proceedings which ensued it was alleged that the underwriters ought to have known (or at least been placed on enquiry) that the money belonged to their client – and that it had been allocated to underwrite a share offer in breach of Section 151 Companies Act 1985 (this section prohibited financial assistance from being given by a company in the acquisition of its own shares).

The underwriters applied to strike out the claim, and the court therefore had to determine if, in this case, they could be held liable as constructive trustees to repay the money, on the basis that they had "knowingly assisted" in the fraud.

The court considered the decision in the Agip case referred to immediately above, and found that a person could not be made liable for "knowing assistance" in the absence of any dishonesty or want of probity on his part – or if knowledge would not have been imported to an "honest and reasonable man".

It thus decided that the underwriters could not have been reasonably expected to question the actions of their client's chief executive. The action to hold them liable failed.

These cases are not particularly recent and others have since shed further light on the issue. The point they illustrate, however, is that whilst a court must apply the existing and clear principles of law in determining whether there has been "knowing assistance" in fraudulent activity, it will also look at each case on its own merits.

Thus your failure to investigate facts that might, or should, raise concerns could incriminate you in one case, but not in another.

1.6 Overseas law and UK companies

The Sarbanes-Oxley Act of the United States ("SOX")

This act came into law in the United States in July 2002 and brought about massive changes in corporate governance in a wide range of areas.

Although it is a US law, its effects reach far beyond those shores – and are still being tested and established today. On the face of it, a literal interpretation means that most of SOX's provisions apply to *any* issuer filing periodic reports with the US's regulator, the Securities and Exchange Commission – including, for example, those UK companies with secondary listings in the US.

The main aim behind SOX was, in the wake of a number of US corporate financial scandals:

- to boost flagging investor confidence in the US stock market;
- to prevent, and punish, corporate and accounting fraud and corruption;
- to assist law enforcers in bringing fraudsters to book; and
- to provide protection for employees bringing incidences of fraud to the authorities' attention of those with responsibility for dealing with it.

Among other things, its practical impact is to:

- increase transparency in terms of companies' financial disclosures;
- increases the accountability of companies' senior executives;
- requires the audit process to be conducted with greater independence than was previously the case; and
- creates new sanctions for wrongdoing by companies' senior executives.

In the specific context of fraud, SOX requires that the Securities and Exchange Commission establish rules requiring companies' in-house and external lawyers to notify their Audit Committee, a committee of independent directors or the board of directors itself, of any material breach of securities law or fiduciary duty where the company's senior executives do not respond in an appropriate way. Lawyers failing to make such notifications are themselves subject to sanctions, and may be disbarred from practice.

1.7 Non-Statutory codes and guidance on fraud risk management

The Combined Code and the Turnbull Committee Report

The "Combined Code" is mandatory only for listed companies – but its provisions are followed by many other organisations, both private and public sector, which are not listed but which want to apply and demonstrate high standards of internal governance and control.

It deals with companies' internal controls in areas such as:

- Financial controls;
- Operational management;
- Compliance; and
- Risk management.

The Turnbull Committee Report on Internal Controls was drafted to provide directors of listed companies with guidance on how to implement the Combined Code requirements on internal controls. Thus, those businesses and their boards which want to demonstrate their high standards of internal control, will often rely on the Combined Code and on Turnbull, for guidance on how to achieve this.

Turnbull, published a year after PIDA, also deals with issues of whistleblowing. In particular it recommends, as part of its guidance to boards on risk management, that companies should adopt whistleblowing policies (and so goes slightly further than PIDA).

1.8 Conclusion

Having considered what constitutes a fraud, and the trends in fraud which have prompted much legislative change, we have then looked very briefly at some of the legislation, case law and guidance which is currently relevant. We will return in more detail to some of these laws later in the book, considering how it applies in practice.

Different Types of Fraud

2.1 General

As we have already said, the term "fraud" is used in different ways – there are the legal definitions as set out in the Fraud Act, and then there are likely to be other events which – whilst they may not meet any of the technical definitions laid down by law – meet our criteria for requiring all of the following:

- Deception;
- Dishonesty and intent; and
- Materiality of that deception.

For the purposes of this text, we will focus our attention on the common use of the term: that is,

- theft (i.e. the deliberate removal of cash or assets to which the fraudster is not entitled); or
- false accounting (i.e. the corruption or falsification of records in order to create a misleading impression).

2.2 General introduction to fraud typologies

There are various different ways of categorising fraud, and within each of these, many different types of specific fraud. Because there is no standard protocol for categorising frauds, some activities span a number of categories – the aim here is simply to alert you to the types of activity which may be carried on under each classification:

- *Internal vs. External* – that is, contrasting frauds against a business/its customers carried on by employees or officers of the company, with those carried on by third parties, including customers themselves.
- *Corporate vs. non-corporate frauds.* Corporate frauds are generally described as those carried out by a number of perpetrators within an organisation as a whole, often on the face of it for the benefit of the organisation (although almost invariably also for their own benefit, for example by increasing their bonuses or retaining their jobs as a result of falsified perceptions of their performance). They might include:

27

- False accounting, including the inflation of profits or the improper timing of accounting for receivables/costs
- The use of elaborate schemes to hide liabilities rather than recognising them on balance sheet

We will look at some examples of such frauds later in the text.

- *Whitecollar vs. non-whitecollar frauds.* Whitecollar frauds are generally regarded as those carried out through the use of false or doctored documentation, whether electronic or hard copy. The term arises from the stereotyped image of an office-worker or professional person in collar and tie, and is often used to capture such events as:
  - Various types of false accounting;
  - Advance fee fraud;
  - Hidden related-party transactions.

  As often as not, white collar crime is also internal – clerical and professional fraudsters perhaps having most access to, and knowledge of, their own employers as to/of any other organisation.
- *Organised crime vs.* ad hoc *frauds.* One of the key factors identified in the rising tide of fraud incidences is a surge in organised criminals engaging in fraud. In many cases this involves criminal groups infiltrating a target organisation (perhaps by having one of their number apply for a job there), or by intimidating existing employees and compelling them to provide information, data or assistance with a scheme. A key area of concern for the authorities is the targeting of vulnerable businesses by groups intent on using the proceeds of their frauds to fund terrorist activities.
- *Banking fraud vs. other types of fraud.* These include:
  - Electronic frauds (see below);
  - Identify theft in order to open, or gain access to, accounts in someone else's name;
  - Cheque fraud; and
  - Credit and debit card frauds.
- *Electronic vs. non-electronic fraud.* Electronic frauds might include:
  - Hacking into a banking system to access funds or information improperly;
  - Email scams;
  - The use of viruses or other software to propagate unauthorised transactions or data transfers.

Non-electronic frauds are all those which do not rely on electronic communications to be perpetrated – false expense claims, the submission of false invoices, and so on.

2.3   Some examples of specific frauds

Having considered some common fraud categorisations, we will now consider some specific fraud events. The following are examples of the most common frauds you may come across:

Theft (or "asset misappropriation")

This may take a variety of guises, including:

- The submission of inflated or false expenses claims;
- The theft or alteration of cheques;
- Fraudulent transfers into bank accounts;
- Collusion with customers and suppliers, for example resulting in overstated purchase invoices;
- Sale of the organisation's assets at an undervalue;
- Employees trading for their own account.

Fraudulent accounting

This may be carried out at a divisional/regional level when reporting up to senior management or the board – for example to boost local bonuses and profit-related rewards or to conceal losses. Alternatively it may be seen at the highest level, in order to create an impression of corporate profitability or to encourage lenders or investors to commit funds.

Purchasing fraud

This is the term used to describe the activities of an employee doing any of the following:

- Authorising orders to a particular supplier in return for bribes;
- Favouring a supplier in which he has a financial interest;
- Over-invoicing or invoicing for fictitious goods (also an example of accounting fraud).

Corruption

This is not, technically, a fraud in some people's lexicons: nevertheless, many examples of corruption involve promoting a false or misleading impression so as to gain some personal or business advantage. These may include:

- Abusing one's position with the business or in other regards, in order to obtain a benefit for oneself or others.
- Bribery of government or other officials to obtain a benefit.
- The theft of customer information.
- Theft of other proprietary or confidential information such as intellectual property, pricing schedules, business plans and the like.
- Identity theft (on which see more below).

Identity theft

This is the term used when a dishonest individual or group obtains someone else's personal details, without their authority, in order to gain some financial or other benefit. Often, the result is to leave the genuine owner of that identity with significant debts, a negative credit history and in some cases with difficult legal hurdles to redressing matters. Identity information may be obtained in a number of ways:

- theft, including theft of mail from the individual's mailbox at home or via the postal service;
- by going through garbage bins and obtaining discarded correspondence;
- through telephone scams;
- over the Internet, by hacking or via email scams.

In such cases the following items of data may assist the fraudster in assuming third party's identity:

- date of birth;
- address (verified using utilities bills such as telephone, gas, water and rate notices);
- passport, driving license or Armed Forces ID numbers;
- National Identity Card, Social Security or Tax Identification Numbers – in those countries which use them;
- banking details, including account numbers, balances and patterns of usage;
- tax records;
- other financial documents.

They may be used to empty the account of the true owner, or alternatively to open new accounts in his name or obtain credit/goods in his name.

Insurance fraud

On the face of it a fraud not only against insurance companies, but also affecting other companies (who are clients of insurers) through the higher premiums the insurers must charge to compensate themselves for fraudulent claims. The fraudulent claims may relate to events which have not in fact happened at all – or may overstate the loss which has arisen to the insured.

In a report published by Norwich Union (NU) in 2005, "The Fraud Report – Shedding Light on Hidden Crime", NU raised the issue of criminal gangs becoming increasingly involved in organised insurance fraud (particularly motor insurance). It cited gangs which sought to "defraud insurers and consumers by submitting high volumes of false . . . claims for damaged vehicles, personal injury and associated loses of earnings and suffering", and expressed the view that this is now the fastest growing area of organised motor fraud.

Advance fee fraud

A term used for a variety of scams where the victim is persuaded to make payments, initially of relatively small amounts of money, with the promise of receiving a much larger amount. Examples include "Nigerian Fee Frauds" (so called because of the number of frauds of this type which appear to have come out of that country), and "419 frauds".

The fraud usually involves:

- the fraudster's contacting the victim (often by email or fax, but sometime also by letter) with a claim that he represents a third party, or the estate of a deceased individual;
- the fraudster will claim that he is aware of significant funds – often cited as being in the many millions of pounds or (more usually) dollars – being held in an account in the name of that party;
- he will claim that he requires the assistance of the victim to secure the release of the funds;
- this assistance is likely to involve the victim's sending details of his own bank account, and/or a sum of money which is small in comparison with

the funds which are allegedly tied up (it may however be quite a significant sum to the victim);

- the victim will be promised a cut of the alleged funds to compensate him for his time and effort. This may be a significant sum, but will never materialise;
- the victim may be told that he has been selected on the basis of his integrity and reputation (on grounds that the rightful owner of the alleged funds, for whom he is securing their release, can trust him to pass them on);
- the victim may be sworn to secrecy on grounds (for example) that he could imperil the safety of the rightful owner. If this tactic is successful it can earn the fraudster valuable time in making off with any money sent to him;
- If the victim sends the initially–requested sum, he is quite likely to be told that complications have arisen requiring that more money is sent. Whether or not he continues to co-operate, he is unlikely to see the return of the money he has already sent, or of the expected millions.
- In some cases, individuals or employees of businesses who have discovered that they have fallen victim to a fraud have – instead of going to the police, and perhaps from a sense of embarrassment – taken matters into their own hands and tried to track down the perpetrators to recoup their money. One or two have suffered considerable violence in so doing, demonstrating that whilst the fraudsters may on the face of it be cowardly individuals, carrying out their business at distance by fax and email, they are capable of considerable brutality to protect themselves.

Such scams are well known by those in certain industries (certain subsets of the finance industry, for example, will receive regular training on how to spot such frauds). Nonetheless, they are a popular tool for fraudsters who manage to ensnare a depressing number of individuals with this scam on a regular basis – in part because of the massive volume of "fishing" contacts made – huge numbers of emails, faxes and letters can be pumped out very cheaply by professional fraudsters, and only a relatively small percentage of individuals need respond for it to be a cost-effective ploy.

Prime bank instrument fraud

Prime Bank Frauds also typically involve claims that the scheme is so secret few are permitted to know about it. To stop the prospective investor from performing proper checks on the scheme, they are usually told that they will be given access to "private markets" between banks – but that they cannot speak to personnel at those banks directly.

Often a power of attorney, which may have been drafted by a legitimate adviser such as a lawyer, will be used in connection with the bank account, the aim being to convince the prospective investor that reputable parties are involved in the structuring, and that their money will consequently be in safe hands.

Fraudulent salesmen of such schemes use a variety of terms of jargon, some with their roots in the real world (standby letters of credit, for example, are often cited and are genuinely used for a variety of reasons – but not for the investment purposes for which they are touted in these cases). They may promote an investment programme using:

- Standby letters of credit;
- Prime bank notes;
- Prime Bank Guarantees;
- Deep-discounted debentures;
- Guaranteed letters of credit;

and they may discuss using these instruments singly, or as part of a "rolling programme of investments". Typically, the salesman will promise annual returns of the order of 40–100 per cent.

In most cases, the key to establishing the scheme's credibility – and thereby successfully conning the investor – is the involvement of a legitimate and licensed bank, broker or law firm. But in many cases, organisations do not check out the parties and relationships as closely as they should, their greed or wish to be seen to have performed well in managing the business' money outweighing their common sense.

Such schemes are nothing new: in fact an example of such a fraud, dating from the early 1990s, in which the Salvation Army itself became victim, is set out in Chapter 5 – External Frauds. Indeed so prevalent are such schemes that the International Chamber of Commerce launched a world-wide awareness-raising campaign in 1996, to alert investors and the banking industry to them. It called sales of these instruments "the financial crime of the century".

Cheque fraud

This involves using a company's cheques to obtain some financial advantage, for example:

- Altering the cheque (payee/amount) without appropriate authority;
- Stealing legitimate cheques written by the company's authorised signatories, and subsequently altering or converting them;

33

- Duplication or counterfeiting of cheques;
- Depositing a cheque into a third-party account without authority;
- Paying a cheque to the company, knowing that insufficient funds are in the account to cover it.

Some commentators also include the use of false invoices to solicit legitimate cheques under this heading, although arguably this is in fact purchasing fraud. Cheque fraud may be carried out either by employees, or by external parties.

2.4 What types of fraud is your business most vulnerable to?

This question may depend on a number of factors:

- *Nature of business.* The nature of a given business will dictate the types of fraud to which it is most vulnerable; those areas of greatest activity are often those in which frauds – particularly low value, high incidence frauds of the type considered by some employees not to be frauds at all – are prevalent. (On the other hand in some more evolved organisations, these are the areas where the best monitoring systems have been developed; consequently incidences of fraud manifest themselves in the quieter, more inactive areas).

  Thus, a relatively high proportion of organisations engaged in retailing suffer purchasing fraud; and many financial services businesses have suffered frauds involving fraudulent transfers of cash.

  In addition, the "job" of being involved in fraud is a highly dynamic one: fraudsters are constantly working on new avenues to exploit, and will naturally focus on the softest targets open to them. Some industries and technologies lend themselves more to this type of abuse than others – in considering a business' fraud risk, you should include an assessment of these factors. Where are the weak links in your system? Is your organisation likely to be targeted because it is, itself, a weak link due to the nature of its activities and the openness of its systems?

  A further factor which is a function of the nature of the organisation's business, is whether it is in an industry which has a culture of open information sharing and co-operation to combat fraud.

  The financial services sector provides some excellent examples of inter industry co-operation: a number of industry bodies have information-sharing networks to which they contribute, and from which they can access, data on individuals or addresses potentially associated with frauds. For example:

- The major credit reference agencies, to which most lending banks subscribe, are members of a network called "GAIN" (the Gone Away Information Network), to which lending organisations provide information on their borrower customers who have moved address without providing a forwarding address.

- "CIFAS" (the Credit Industry Fraud Advisory Service) – www.cifas. org.uk – is a fraud prevention service to which member organisations can subscribe, then sharing information on best practice to avoid frauds – but also, again, information relating to individuals or addresses. When a member becomes aware of a fraud, it flags a warning against the relevant address to which the account, or application, relates. This does not necessarily mean that the associated individual is himself a fraudster (after all, his identity could have been stolen) – but it does mean that other members know to take extra care when dealing with applications linked to that name/address.

Other industries are also beginning to co-operate and share information in similar ways, to help reduce the incidence of fraud on their sectors as a whole: but the financial services sector is perhaps the most evolved in this regard, essentially because being a "money" industry it is highly targeted by fraudsters.

- *Size of business.* Similarly, size can be a factor; the simple volume of transactions can make it easier for frauds to slip through the net unnoticed. In addition, as businesses get bigger their activities become more process-driven (that is to say, the high volume of relatively routine transactions becomes carried out in accordance with a set of standardised procedures – rather than being individually handled – and if there are no obvious alarm bells, then this process-oriented environment can enable more seemingly routine, but in fact fraudulent, transactions to be undertaken without much scrutiny). The more process-driven a business becomes, the more it lends itself to a certain type of fraudster, particularly if that fraudster is familiar with those processes and with the levels at which any extra scrutiny will kick in on an "exceptions" basis.

Many larger businesses also suffer purchasing fraud, for example by way of the submission of invoices for fictitious goods and services, or where the invoiced amount has been inflated.

- *Management engagement and commitment to implementation.* Firms which are underinvested in terms of time, resource and commitment to combating fraud are, unsurprisingly, more vulnerable to frauds than those which take it seriously. The allocation of responsibility for fraud risk management, and the development and implementation of a fraud mitigation plan, to a senior (often board-level) individual or team is key to improving visibility, accountability and ultimately results; as is the allocation of people, training and budgets to implementing the plan. Fraud risk management should also become part of the project in developing any new products, processes or markets; where it is embedded early in the process, results are likely to be much improved compared to where it happens late in the planning process.
- *Culture.* Highly coloured by management's level of commitment, a business' overall culture can be a critical defence in the fight against fraud. Culture is invariably influenced from the top, with the integrity and values of the business being exemplified through the words and actions of its senior executives; but recruitment is also important, as is training (both formal and informal) and the use of different communications media to propagate high standards of integrity, alertness and accountability at all levels within the firm. Firms with lax values, or a flabby compliance culture where lip-service only is paid to procedures, will find that their customers' and their own assets are equally vulnerable to abuse, both by staff and – in the absence of staff vigilance – by outsiders.
- *Maturity.* Businesses can, without doubt, "learn" from experience – although that learning manifests itself initially through the learning of their employees, and then through the way in which this is translated into better fraud risk management, through improved systems and controls. This translation into better risk management can only take place if the management commitment and cultural issues exist to support it; sadly as we saw in Chapter 1, a disappointing number of businesses and their managers do seem unable to learn from their fraud experiences – or perhaps, believe that it is more cost-effective to set their tolerance for frauds at such a level that a number do slip through, but business can continue unimpeded.

Analytical Methods in Fraud
Risk Management

3.1 Planning

Having determined who is responsible for the identification of fraud risk in an organisation (and there may well be more than one party or division responsible for this), it is important to plan the approach thoroughly.

A planned approach, with appropriate synthesis and analysis of data trends, and assessment data in the context of other information, can provide a significant improvement on the more basic approach of simply testing and verifying the current figures, as presented at a given point. The fact that numbers are inconsistent with the trend, or with what should be expected, should act as a valuable flag to instigate further investigation.

The process of designing the plan will generally run along the following lines:

- Gather information about the business, sufficient to identify where there are risks of material mis-statements due to fraud;
- Assess these risks, having taken into account the business' internal controls and systems; and
- Respond to these risks, on a prioritised basis (that is, recommending an action plan to deal with these risks – taking into account the likelihood and impact of the risk – and monitoring its implementation).

From the above, it should be clear that a key element of any worthwhile fraud risk management plan is the identification of key fraud risk factors. These are factors which, whilst not necessarily indicating that fraud exists, should act as a warning sign that it may.

Let us think a little more deeply about each stage of the process we have identified above.

3.2 Gathering information about the business

This part of the process will involve gaining a clear understanding of all relevant processes taking place in the business – both in their documented form (e.g. what the procedures manual says should happen) and in their actual form (what people actually do on a day to day basis, which may be very different).

The process should then involve an assessment of what controls are in place to ensure that procedures are adhered to, and if/how the assets of the business or its customers may be put at risk.

Approaches to this element can vary, depending on the nature, scale and complexity of the business. For example:

- Invariably, the risk assessor should begin by reviewing documented and actual procedures, and analysing for himself where the vulnerabilities may be;
- He should spend time interviewing the management within each division/department in order to gain insight into their awareness, and understanding, of the fraud risks within their area. This may also reveal a need to educate the managers themselves!
- Any risk assessment should also include discussions with internal and external audit, and with the audit committee itself if the organisation has established one. For financial services organisations, discussions with the designated MLRO can also be helpful, because of the often close alignment between money laundering and fraud.
- Discussions with in-house legal advisers may also be worthwhile, especially if these individuals are involved in assisting in recoveries: they may have valuable insights into weaknesses in the process, or trends;
- Further insight is often to be gained from one-to-one discussions with the team members responsible for carrying out or supervising each stage of the process. These individuals are often aware of weaknesses in the system, but have hitherto done nothing because they do not perceive it to be their remit to do so – or indeed, may have called attention to the deficiency but been ignored;
- Additional insight can often be obtained from informal discussion with a wider range of employees. One approach to this involves gathering members of the operational team together and brainstorming those areas where they see opportunities for frauds to occur, and/or to be concealed. The value of this is often in its informality, and in harnessing the creativity of employees (some of whom, though undoubtedly honest, have a cheerful ability to think like criminals when called upon to do so!). A useful approach is to encourage them to put themselves in the shoes of a would-be fraudster – for example:
  - As the accountant/book-keeper for this division, how could you embezzle money and cover your tracks?
  - If you were the Chief Executive Officer, in what ways could you inflate profits/improve the financial statements to impress shareholders, increase your bonus, or encourage a bank to lend to the business?

- If you worked in the loading bay, how could you thieve stock from us without getting caught?
- It is worth noting that whilst many risk managers, especially those from an audit background, tend to focus on individuals involved in the financial reporting process, there are many other points in the organisation at which frauds can be instigated (those involved with taking on new customers, for example, or vetting them for creditworthiness; IT personnel responsible for computer security; and buildings/stock managers responsible for security of various types of asset or inventory).

  If you come from an accounting background yourself, and are responsible for assessing fraud risks, do not be intimidated by your lack of knowledge in areas other than the purely financial – see it as an opportunity to learn more about the business you are involved with, and engage with your colleagues in other areas.
- Do not restrict your enquiries to senior personnel. Frauds – especially internal frauds – may be spotted by anyone, at any level within the organisation – but some employees lower down the ranks may not realise that it is up to them to report concerns, or may not be aware of to whom they can make their report (quite likely, you) – or may be anxious about recriminations and reprisals if they do so.

In addition, however, such employees can be helpful in corroborating (or otherwise!) management's perspective of how things actually happen in practice. Furthermore, asking the same question of different people enables you to compare their responses – and may identify anomalies which present risks otherwise un-noticed.

3.3 Fraud risk factors

Again, in the imprecise science of fraud risk management, there are different views as to what constitutes a "risk" or "risk factor" – but one common method of identifying such a factor is by way of the "fraud risk triangle".

This says that a fraud risk factor is any factor (e.g. a weakness in the system, etc) which incorporates the three conditions of the fraud risk triangle. The fraud risk triangle is predicated on the assumption that fraud occurs when three factors co-exist, and it is represented as follows (Figure 3.1):

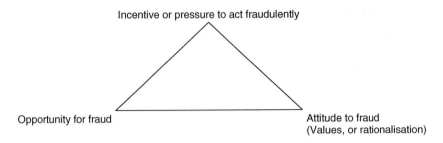

Figure 3.1 The Fraud Risk Triangle

Let us take each of those factors in turn:

- **Incentive**

  For example, individual employees have an incentive to act fraudulently i

  - they are under severe personal financial pressure, either through an accu
    mulation of ordinary "day to day" debt or because of some specific issue
    such as gambling;
  - their greed prompts them to take fraudulent steps to increase their wealth
    even if they are not actually in personal financial difficulty;
  - they are approached by organised criminals who threaten violence to them
    or their families;
  - they are themselves part of such organisations and are seeking to financ
    (for example) terrorist activities;
  - they are part of a management team whose bonus, pay rise or job retentio
    depends on their ability to show increased profits, assets under manage
    ment or some other measure;
  - revenge (for example they perceive themselves to have been wrongl
    passed over for promotion by the organisation or their boss);
  - they are simply thrill-seekers, with no particular need for the money
    or they relish the intellectual challenge. A surprising number of fraud
    (particularly, it must be said, of the electronic variety) are carried ou
    by perpetrators who when questioned, admit that their motivation wa
    simply that they wanted to see if they would "get away with it".

- **Opportunity**

  Opportunity exists if controls are weak or non-existent.

- **Attitude**

  An individual whose values are such that he is able to be dishonest or di
  loyal to further his own interests, or those of an associate, is more predispose
  to fraudulent activity than one whose values centre on honesty and loyalty.

3.4 Assessing the risks, taking account of internal controls

Having identified as many fraud risk factors as is possible, the next task is to asses their:

- Likelihood (how likely is it that the event will occur?); and
- Impact (what is the potential loss to the company if they do occur).

There are various methods of carrying out such an assessment: the key is to adopt a rational, and consistent, approach rather than an "intuitive" (i.e. guesswork) basis. You will only be able to justify the allocation of risk management resources to the appropriate areas, if you have assessed the risks identified on the basis of appropriate metrics.

One approach is to assess:

- the likelihood of the event in terms of the number of times it might be expected to occur, given the current status of systems and controls; and
- the impact of the event in terms of quantifying any such loss as a percentage of annual profit, turnover, or assets.

This should enable you to identify those risks which require prompt and significant remediation, and those which are less urgent or require less resource to mitigate them, or indeed which the business may decide are so remote or minor as to be left unremedied.

The process of logging these assessments can be a daunting task, especially in large or complex businesses: for a medium-sized company transacting business on credit, or internationally, you may have 8 or 10 divisions or functions, and within each of these at least another 8 or 10 specific risks – leading to a matrix of between some 60–100 risks. Many complex organisations will have more; small or simple businesses should have less. The point is that they all need logging, assessing for potential impact/severity, and allocating to an "owner".

- One option is to use standard fraud risk management software (or indeed more general risk management software) on which to capture the identified risks. Some such packages have been written with specific businesses in mind, and come pre-populated with a standard range of risk categories and risks, which can be adapted by the business itself to accommodate its precise circumstances;

- Another option is to establish a database or (in simpler cases) spreadsheet-based matrix, organised so as to sort the identified fraud risks by:
  - Nature;
  - Department/owner;
  - Control or action to remedy (bearing in mind that one control may remedy a number of different fraud risks);
  - Comments from the department manager/risk owner;
  - Additional comments;

  and including columns for later population, to show the action by date, progress update, and completed/uncompleted status.

3.5   Involving the management team

Because responsibility for implementing any remedial action is likely to sit in the business, as opposed to with the Risk Manager, it is important to keep the management team as involved as is possible, without diverting them unreasonably from their day-to-day business objectives.

In addition, of course, involving divisional managers can yield useful information as to how the processes have been established, what supervisory arrangements are in place, how exceptions and significant transactions are handled, and sometimes how actual activity differs from their perception of what is going on!

For this reason it is a good idea to circulate the initial draft of your findings to the managers of the relevant divisions, enabling them to respond with comments or clarifications if they feel that:

- you have misunderstood any part of the process;
- there are additional anti-fraud safeguards in place to mitigate the fraud risk identified (which perhaps were not known to the particular employee you initially interviewed);
- they believe the remedial action is disproportionate to the risk, and have some alternative proposal; or
- in some cases, they believe the risk is actually greater than that identified and wish to escalate or accelerate the remediation.

3.6 Responding to identified fraud indicators/ fraud risks

Having carried out an assessment of the risks and their likely impact/incidence, they may then be divided into the following:

- Those which cannot be tolerated at all and must be eradicated, where this is possible;
- Those which require some mitigating action ("remediation") to reduce or avoid them;
- Those which cannot be mitigated (or only partly so) but against which some other protection can be used – for example, insurance; and
- Those which the company is happy to leave unremediated, at least for the time being, perhaps because their impact is so minor or their likelihood so remote, that any action taken would be disproportionately costly compared with the benefit gained.

Those to be remediated should be prioritised, and remedial action agreed on. The action plan should incorporate:

- The action to be taken;
- The expected outcome in terms of risk mitigation after action (for example, a reduction in the likely incidence and/or severity of the risk factor after treatment, using the standards of measurement we looked at before);
- The time frame for action;
- Who is responsible for implementing the action.

As with logging the identified risks and their likely incidence/severity, monitoring the progress and achievement of these action plans can be challenging in itself, especially with a business which is large or complex. One question which you will need to determine is the accountability for this ongoing monitoring:

- You may find it appropriate to have the risk manager, or alternatively Internal Audit, maintain the database of outstanding actions and chase for progress reports.
- Whoever it is, it is important that they have sufficient authority to seek and obtain appropriate responses on progress from the business divisions themselves – or alternatively, if it falls within their remit (as it may with Internal Audit) to test for progress and completeness themselves.

- In some businesses, responsibility for implementing the proposed actions may rest with the risk manager himself. For many, however, it is more effective to push responsibility back "into the business" so that the management team for each division are required to implement the necessary actions within the stated time frame, or provide a reasonable rationale if they have not done so.
- In any event it is critical that the action plan is taken seriously by all members of the management team – not just by the Risk Manager and/or Internal Audit. You may find it easiest to achieve this if:
  - the action plan is a standing agenda item for Board or Audit Committee meetings; and
  - implementation by the divisional management is seen as contributing to the measurement of their overall performance, so that their rewards package may be affected should they fail to achieve the target without good reason.

3.7 Fraud indicators

Factors which indicate that a fraud may be being attempted or perpetrated (as opposed to there being a high propensity for the risk of this) are usually known as fraud indicators – you may call them by some other name, however, such as fraud alerts, red flags or similar.

In essence they are the alarm bells which should set your whiskers twitching (to mix a metaphor rather inelegantly!) – having:

- identified the various fraud risk factors for your business;
- discussed the potential avenues by which they could be exploited with staff at various levels; and
- put in place action plans to remedy them where appropriate;

you will still wish to have various systems in place to alert senior management/the fraud risk manager that untoward events are underway.

The approach used for this will depend on the nature of the business itself – for example, financial services businesses with appropriately integrated systems may use technology which alerts management to certain patterns of account usage which may be indicative of fraudulent behaviour. For other types of business this automated method of account behavioural analysis may not be possible or even valuable. For each business, you should consider the elements that should indicate that a fraud may be underway.

These could include:

- unusual or suspicious events associated with processing of documentation such as account-opening procedures;
- evasiveness on the part of certain individuals, or an unwillingness to take holidays or allow others to cover their job for them;
- heavy use of certain types of suspense account;
- knowledge of personal financial pressure on certain individuals in financially sensitive positions;
- sudden lack of adherence to standard procedures for sensitive activities (these may include writing of cheques, authorising of payments and the like);
- unhealthily close relationships between employees with influence in sensitive areas, and external customers or suppliers.

You may wish, as part of your fraud risk management process, to establish some formal way of logging such alerts when they are reported to you. A relatively standard way of doing so is as follows:

Motivation	Opportunity	Method	Fraud indicator/Red flag	Method	Consequence
For example Individual employee with gambling debts	For example, poor internal controls over the tendering process	Fraudulent invoicing for services to the organisation	Employee has close relationship with service provider	Preparation of false tender application, and subsequent false invoices for services	Failure to give contract to best provider Overpayment for non-existent services

The process of capturing these events may seem burdensome and time-consuming but such a log can prove invaluable when reviewing vulnerabilities over time.

3.8 Statistical/technological tools in fraud risk analysis

Certain types of business lend themselves to more automated methods of fraud "flagging" – in addition to, as opposed to instead of, the more intuitive methods of relying on employee awareness, robust systems and controls, and proper supervision of activity.

Examples include those industries which are transaction-heavy" – for example, banking and insurance, where specialist software can be used to report on an exceptions-basis patterns of activity which may indicate the presence of frauds. For example:

- Account-monitoring packages can be used which will alert credit card operators to the likelihood that a card has been stolen and is being used by someone other than its true owner. This may be on the basis that the pattern of transactions differs from that which has been registered in the past;
- Some credit-scoring software packages can alert lending institutions to the likelihood that a loan application is potentially fraudulent;
- Several insurance companies have experienced sharp reductions in their claims fraud experience through the use of voice analytical software on their telephone lines (that said, it has also been observed that this reduction in fraud may in part have been due to the warning given to claims callers, that such software was in operation!).

Technological tools are not available, or suitable, for all types of organisation; nor do they provide a substitute for other factors such as a positive anti-fraud culture, strong systems and controls, and a workable whistleblowing policy.

However, they can provide a valuable tool in high turnover environments, wherever the metrics of account activity lend themselves to analysis. It is well worth researching whether there are options available to you.

3.9 Cultural issues in fraud risk management

One aspect which challenges many individuals, charged with the task of running a fraud risk management exercise, is a natural tendency to rely on representations made by their colleagues. (In the case of an external auditor or fraud risk consultant, the need is to suspend any tendency to assume his client – or at least every employee of his client – is honest).

It is important that a fraud risk manager approaches his task with a mindset which combines open-mindedness with a level of scepticism. This can be especially challenging where an auditor relies heavily on a particular client for fee income, or where the relevant employee has previously worked closely with the individuals he is now required to risk-assess: the challenge may be so great as to rule some people out of a potential role in risk evaluation.

That said, the individual should not, and need not, be unduly aggressive or discourteous. An appropriate balance needs to be struck – as one risk manager cheerfully puts it when explaining her approach, "trust – but verify".

In terms of ownership, the ideal corporate culture for the deterrence is as follows:

- Fraud risk management starts at the top: the board and senior managers must be committed to introducing, and maintaining, effective risk management strategies to minimise the risk of fraud;
- That said, fraud risk management is also *everybody's* concern. Every employee has the opportunity to spot matters of concern, and should remain alert and vigilant to potential abuse of the company's assets;
- Whilst people remain accountable for their actions, as far as is possible a "no-blame" culture is cultivated. This means that
  - Employees can draw attention to their concerns over potential frauds without fear of reprisals, and so are more likely to do so;
  - They can also come to management with concerns when they themselves have neglected procedures so as to leave the company vulnerable to fraud (for example by replying to a client's telephone query about his account without verifying that he is who he says he is) – or where they believe they can improve the way they do things in future, so as to minimise the risk of fraud.

When considering the issue of culture and fraud risk management, we should never forget the very real added value of promoting a positive anti-fraud culture within the organisation; employees may often be your greatest risk in terms of fraud – whether as perpetrators, or simply by a lack of alertness or accountability. They can, however, also be your first line of defence.

Section 2

Risks, and the Systems
to Counter Them

Internal Frauds

4.1 Vulnerability to internal frauds

When considering a company's vulnerability to internal frauds (i.e. those perpetrated by its own employees or officers), it is worth going back to the Fraud Risk Triangle – a concept we have met in an earlier chapter.

Remember, the Fraud Risk Triangle proposes that risk is predicated on the existence of three factors:

- *Opportunity* (the company's systems have to be such that they can be circumvented);
- *Motivation* (the fraudster must need or want the cash, assets or other benefit he obtains);
- *Values/ethics/culture* (the fraudster must have a set of values or ethics that predisposes or allows him to attempt fraud; *or* the company's culture must accord with those values).

Let us consider each of these in the context of employees of a business. The employees need:

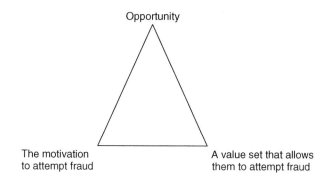

In terms of internal frauds, then, some danger signs include:

Opportunity

- *Poor internal controls* and systems, with many loopholes and a lack of supervision;
- *Failure to remedy* internal control failings on an ongoing basis, especially where remediation would be relatively simple and cost-effective;
- *Lack of segregation of duties* and a failure to impose proper reviews of accounting and other activity;

- *Weaknesses in systems* which can be exploited and result in ineffective reporting/inaccurate or late management information;
- *Little or no verification* of suppliers and the orders placed with them;
- *Overseas subsidiaries of a corporate grouping* which are not subject to proper internal audit or assessment by group senior management.

Values/ethics/culture

- *Culturally, lip-service only, or no prioritisation of* the establishment of proper internal controls (a "we have to be *seen* to toe the line" approach);
- *One or two senior individuals* dominating the business, in such a way that their activities cannot be properly overseen;
- *A relaxed approach to breaches*, circumvention of controls and the like;
- *Secrecy – employees insisting on sole control* and communication with a given customer or supplier, and being secretive about dealings with the customer or supplier;
- *Employees* with wide-ranging external business interests which may conflict or compete with their obligations to the organisation and its stakeholders.

Motivation

- *Employees who are under personal financial pressure* – for example, they are not earning enough to manage on or have mounting debt problems;
- *Employees who are under pressure to show good performance* either because it will affect their financial reward package/job security, *or* because they are personally concerned to be seen in a good light by their peers, bosses, spouse or others;
- *Employees whose lifestyles* appear excessively lavish in the context of their known remuneration and other sources of income – are they under pressure to continue to appear "successful", and are therefore having trouble cutting back?
- *Senior employees being rewarded lavishly*, whilst more junior ones are perhaps underpaid in comparison – does this create a sense that it is "unfair"?

Having recognised these factors, we will now look at some of the typical internal frauds you may encounter – and the strategies that may help mitigate the above factors, and reduce the risk of the frauds occurring.

4.2   Some typical internal frauds

Time and space can only permit us to look at a small sample of the many and often creative frauds carried on by employees against their employers: but the strategies for preventing these examples will, in most cases, prevent abuse in other types of fraud.

Purchasing fraud

Purchasing frauds are a good example of a category of fraud sometimes referred to as "salami frauds". This is because whilst each slice of the salami (that is, each individual sum defrauded) is relatively small, the entirety (the whole salami) can amount to a considerable sum. One not-uncommon example of a purchasing fraud falling into this category (and taken from real life) is as follows.

A company established a new distribution warehouse, and at the same point, decided to outsource its vehicle transport arrangements. The transport manager was charged with soliciting tenders for this part of the process – to be reviewed and considered by a committee which was independent of the transport function. As part of this process, each applicant for the tender was asked to quote on the basis of providing vehicles for specified journeys; and in addition, to quote a rate for extra journeys over and above this "core" requirement.

The contract was duly awarded to an applicant firm. During the following few years, the transport manager and the external supplier colluded to approve invoices for fictitious journeys, all of which were invoiced to the company at the contractually-agreed rate; they shared the proceeds of these non-existent journeys.

This particular fraud was allowed to remain undiscovered when the company went through its initial comparison of actual figures against budgets, because the initial budgets for the startup phase of the new arrangement were not particularly detailed – and the senior management had expected some considerable variances at outset whilst teething problems were ironed out (i.e. whilst the company's distribution was moved from the old warehouse to the new one). Further, by the time things had settled down, the budget included a certain number of fictitious journeys as part of the anticipated cost base – they had become built into the budget.

This highlights the need for the following:

- Care during times of disruption, which might be used to disguise the establishment of a fraudulent scheme. You may want to consider putting in extra checks and controls at such times;
- Insufficiently rigorous challenges from the finance department on how budgets have been based;
- A lack of zero-based budgeting;
- Limited ongoing monitoring of activity – in particular of long-term or high value contracts;
- A lack of independent challenge by the finance department on the issue of transport costs relative to other relevant data (e.g. sales);
- A single individual having the main or sole contact with a major supplier;
- Potentially, lifestyle factors indicating that the individual is living beyond the means expected of his normal pay;
- Also, potentially, signs of the supplier providing the employee with lavish entertainment or hospitality.

Accounting fraud

Typical accounting frauds include:

- *Suspense accounts* being overused in the course of the year (even if they are closed out at the company's year-end (y/e));
- *Accruals being manipulated* inappropriately for the business (for example, to inflate profits in a particular year so as to meet targets and secure a bonus);
- *Round amounts of* significant debit postings, prepayments, carry-forwards and so on, which may indicate some relatively crude attempts at fraud;
- *The Sales Ledger* being kept open after the financial y/e cut-off to accommodate the recording of sales which should properly fall into the next year;
- *Understatement of accruals and provisions.*

Warning signs or increased risk factors can include:

- *A system which itself allows* ledgers to be kept open after y/e, especially where this allows inclusion of post y/e income but associated costs are excluded;
- *The use of accounting policies* which are not in accordance with industry/group standards and/or are inconsistently applied;

- *Pressure on management* to achieve quick results and/or meet demanding targets: senior management should consider whether its remuneration policies are appropriate or encourage fraud.

Employees, especially those responsible for the establishment of new divisions or outlying branches, may also feel under pressure to demonstrate inflated profits or a more robust balance sheet than is actually the case, by:

- Aggressive accounting policies or policies that are frequently changed;
- The deferring or capitalisation of expenses;
- The recognition of revenues (including cut-off);
- The over-valuation of assets.

Remedial action can include.

- Robust review of new or remote branch offices;
- Provision of internal audit resource to visit such new operations;
- Frequent reconciliation of cash flow against reported profit to identify mismatches.

HR fraud

The types of fraud which may be encountered under this heading include:

- Carrying out work for other parties on company time;
- Claiming sick days when not actually unwell;
- Claiming to be in the office (and perhaps claiming hourly pay or overtime) when not actually there.

The main protections against this type of fraud are

- Proper recruitment policies to limit the intake of dishonest staff;
- Leading by example – senior management not being seen to "swing the lead";
- Reasonable vigilance – (though it may be counterproductive to make this unduly aggressive: if people are treated as though they are not trustworthy, they may decide to behave in that fashion);
- An environment in which staff can whistleblow without fear of reprisals;
- Entry systems that log individual employee access to and from the building;
- Periodic testing of claimed hours – for example, if someone routinely claims to be in at their desk at 6 a.m., verifying on a number of days that this is so;

- Routine review of the activities people are undertaking (you may need to ensure that this is provided for in your IT security policy) – for example that staff are forewarned that their computers may be remotely monitored as a matter of course;
- The requirement that sick days are evidenced by a doctor's note, and/or sick pay policies that allow for reasonable support of the genuinely sick, but which are set at such a level as to encourage people back to work.

Electronic banking frauds

These may involve the theft of company or customer money using the company's electronic banking system. The following example, taken from real life, shows how careless controls can provide the opportunity for such frauds.

The accounts supervisor of the victim company (a chemicals manufacturer) managed to defraud his employer of some £1m over a period of some 2 years – at a rate of approximately £50,000 per month. His rationale was that he had a serious gambling habit, was running up debts and could not service them.

The accounts supervisor was not himself one of the "designated holders" of the two banking payment authentication devices required to authorise and effect a payment. However, he managed to get hold of both, since neither was kept in a safe or locked drawer (they were left in an unlocked desk drawer).

The password of the first, he obtained by looking over the shoulder of the authorised user when that user was authorising legitimate payments. He obtained the other because its authorised holder had written his password on the operational manual that accompanied it. Using these passwords and the devices in tandem, he was able to effect payments away for his own benefit.

The payments escaped discovery for some time because the fraudster was himself responsible for the bank account reconciliations. He concealed them by altering the formula for totalling columns in the reconciliations spreadsheets.

In the accounts themselves, he set debit amounts against credits in the purchase ledger, expense accounts and suspense accounts. The expense accounts themselves were subject to no very robust monitoring.

This sad catalogue of poor controls only came to an end when the fraudster tried to make a more-than-usually sizeable payment, to pay off a large gambling debt.

The types of controls that should be in place to protect against similar frauds include:

- Keeping electronic payment authentication devices in a locked drawer or safe;
- Ensuring that passwords are kept securely and are confidential to the user;
- It may be possible to enforce some form of monitoring, which would pick up incidences where the payee bank account is the same as an employee's bank account (as it was in this case);
- Similarly, sufficient second review/scrutiny to pick up that the payee details were the same as, or very similar to, the employees;
- Ensure sufficient segregation of activities and duties, so that the individual responsible for making payments is not also the person who reconciles the bank accounts (although admittedly this would not have helped in this particular case);
- Senior management review of the bank accounts and reconciliations;
- Robust review of the balance sheet from time to time;
- Better budget monitoring and supervision so that those accountable for expense items have the opportunity to pick up that unauthorised or fictitious expenses have been put through.
- Periodic audit of spreadsheets to identify amendments that have been made to any formulae.

Goods shipping fraud

It is not unheard of for employees to divert goods being shipped to a customer, to their own home addresses instead. The best protections against such frauds are to:

- Screen shipping addresses against known employee addresses (but bear in mind that they may have selected the address of a friend or relative instead);
- Ensure that you have an audit system to monitor and record any changes to shipping addresses, and that the reasons for these are reviewed periodically.

Assisting or colluding with external fraudsters

We should not forget that in many cases, employees are not the key perpetrators themselves – but have been bribed, threatened or otherwise pressured to collude with external fraudsters. We will look at examples of external frauds in Chapter 5.

Having considered some common types of fraud (Section 1), the warning signs that might alert us to an incidence of internal fraud, and some specific steps that might have prevented each – we will now move on to look at a more general range of fraud risk management approaches that should help limit the incidence of internal fraud.

Sensible steps include the establishment of:

- *Sound internal controls* which should be periodically reviewed both by senior management and by the Internal Audit department;
- *Internal Audit departments* and similar, which should be adequately resourced to cope with the planned workload for the year ahead;
- *A fraud awareness training programme* for all staff, highlighting what to look out for and what steps to take should an employee become suspicious that a fraud has, or may be, committed;
- *Effective fraud reporting lines and mechanisms.* For example, it may be appropriate to designate a board-level individual (such as a Non-Executive Director) as the responsible individual to whom any such suspicions should be referred. Where this is done, the identity of the responsible individual, and the procedure for making a report, should be communicated to all staff;
- *The extension of policies and procedures, and review/internal audit mechanisms* to overseas branches and subsidiaries. Management should ensure that it is familiar with local office procedures, and any variations from standard group policies;
- *The identification of vulnerable assets* and the taking of appropriate steps to protect them (for example, proper control of account signatories: the identification and tagging of high-value, portable items such as laptops);
- *Robust recruitment and staff vetting procedures.* A business whose staff are known to be honest from the outset, and indeed whose identities have has been verified, is less likely to be vulnerable to internal frauds. Credit checks may reveal those potential recruits whose financial situation might make it wise to keep them in a non-financially sensitive role;
- *A policy which promotes a culture of active staff accountability.* The company may wish to implement a policy which sets out its attitude to fraud and encourages staff to adopt an alert and proactive approach;
- *A policy which prevents the victimisation of whistleblowers.* The company may wish to ensure its policy embeds a measure of protection for "whistleblowers": for example, by ensuring that reports can be made anonymously and/or by outlawing the harassment of those who have made reports;

- *An active approach to dealing with suspicions of fraud* – for example, by ensuring that suspicion reports are followed up promptly;
- *A positive culture of adherence to normal company procedures* – for example, the enforcement of any annual leave entitlements. It is not unusual for employees who are involved in frauds to be unwilling to absent themselves from the office, in case the fraud should be uncovered in their absence;
- *An alertness to unusual employee behaviour patterns.* The possible reluctance to take leave which we have noted above is only one possible example. We have already touched on others, but obvious ones include:
  - A lifestyle which appears, on the face of it, to be beyond the means of the employee based on what is known of his income and circumstances;
  - Secretiveness with regard to particular clients or business contacts; reluctance to delegate work to others or share;
  - Behaviour which seems generally irrational.

External Frauds

5.1 Introduction

External frauds are those perpetrated against the business by people other than its employees/officers. These people could include:

- Customers of the business;
- Counterparties such as suppliers;
- Unconnected parties, such as identity thieves setting up fraudulent accounts or relationships;
- Professional fraudsters, including organised criminals.

Examples of external frauds are numerous (though perhaps not as numerous as those of internal frauds, due to the depressing preponderance of frauds by employees and management of companies). We will take a look at some categories:

5.2 Supplier frauds

Many larger organisations are at risk of supplier fraud – sometimes facilitated by collusion on the part of an internal employee. Examples of supplier fraud can include:

- Suppliers invoicing for bogus supplies;
- Suppliers overbilling/double billing, albeit for consignments of goods which were actually sent;
- Supplier bribery and corruption of the company's employees, so as to secure preferential treatment in any tender process or to secure supply contracts regardless of the competitiveness of their offering;
- Suppliers who have been paid in advance disappearing with the money;
- The substitution of inferior goods for those originally contracted for.

Among the best defences against such frauds are

- Careful vetting of new suppliers;
- Proper audit and, where appropriate, occasional sampling of the goods supplied to ensure that not only quantity, but quality and provenance is as billed for;
- A full periodic reconciliation of supplier payments against goods inward;
- Thorough checking of goods, especially electronic ones, including any barcode attachments;
- Care when considering paying new suppliers in advance, or allowing advance payments to creep up for even long-standing suppliers;

- Care where the employees responsible for goods inwards (warehousemen, payments department) have unusually close relationships with suppliers;
- Where any tender process is used, an audit to ensure that this has been properly conducted;
- Prompt investigation of any complaints by other suppliers that they seem unable to secure orders, regardless of the competitiveness or quality of their product.

5.3 Customer frauds

The nature of customer frauds will vary widely with the nature of the business. For companies engaged in retail supply of goods to customers, examples include:

- Customers falsely alleging that the goods they have ordered have arrived damaged;
- Customers falsely alleging non-delivery of their orders;
- Customers taking receipt of goods, making use of them and then returning them – falsely alleging that they are unused (sometimes a problem in the clothing industry and with some electrical goods);
- Counterfeit cash (especially if your store takes euros and your staff are not familiar with all of the different designs) and forged gift vouchers;
- Customer bribery or corruption of the company's employees, in order to secure some benefit such as discounts, excessive "free samples" or similar;
- Refund fraud, where the fraudster returns goods which he has stolen from the store, sometimes accompanied by the till receipt from an earlier genuine purchase (whether his or someone else's) and sometimes claiming to have lost the receipt or been given the item as a gift;
- Customer cheque and credit card fraud.

Some such frauds, for example smaller cases of failure to return goods erroneously supplied, can be difficult to prove, and many organisations take the view that to attempt to do so would be unduly damaging to their general goodwill. Others take a more rigorous line, arguing that a high incidence of fraud costs all customers unfairly, through the cost to the company and consequent high prices it entails.

Cheque and payment card fraud are particularly prevalent in the retail and catering trades. Some standard steps can help to reduce the risk, however:

- Careful observation of the customer as he signs the slip, if you are still in a non-Chip-and-Pin environment (still the case for some businesses!), or keys in his number. Look out for any signs of nervousness;
- Check the start and expiry dates on the card;
- Check the card itself – is there any sign that it has been tampered with?
- Where appropriate, telephone for authorisations and if need be ask for additional identification;
- Do not stick to the same authorisation level for your outlet indefinitely – fraudsters can learn what these are through experience and exploit them;
- Make good use of lists of stolen cards published by the police or card issuers;
- Be particularly careful of buyers who appear to be choosing the goods they want to buy without much care (this may indicate they are not buying for themselves, or at their own expense, and plan to sell on the fraudulently-purchased goods promptly);
- Have, use and display prominently CCTV equipment – this can be a powerful deterrent;
- It may be helpful to let the customer see you are making these checks. If he is holding a stolen card, he may lose his nerve and flee.

Customer credit fraud may also involve the establishment of a credit account using stolen or forged identity details (in the manner discussed in Chapter 2).

- The use of verification services such as Experian, or of inter-business facilities such as GAIN and CIFAS (see also Chapter 2) can help reduce the incidence of such events;
- If you are performing your own verification checks, ask for at least two items to evidence identity (many fraudsters find it easy to obtain one verifiable set of ID – but two documents can prove more of a challenge);
- Do not rely on easily-forged or hard to verify documents. Insist on recognisable documents issued by a known entity such as a utilities provider, government department or financial institution.

To minimise refund fraud, you should:

- Insist on till receipts before accepting items for refund;
- Only accept returns in their original packaging;

- Ask for the customer's name and address, and some proof of identity (not only may this scare a fraudster off – it will also enable you to monitor "serial refunders"). You may be able to do this by offering to send the refund cheque in the mail to the customer's home;
- Consider offering credit notes instead of cash back as an alternative, especially if there is no till receipt but you do not want to risk losing too much customer goodwill.

In all of these areas, there is no substitute for good staff training and alertness: you may find it beneficial to reward staff whose vigilance results in frauds being thwarted, and/or to recognise them in internal company publications.

5.4 Embezzlement

Whilst not a subset of fraud in itself, it is worth examining the term "embezzlement", since it is used in a variety of ways. Its proper definition is of a fraud where someone comes by property legally, and then converts it for his own use.

There is therefore a good argument for saying that when the embezzler comes by the property (knowing that it rightfully belongs to others) he owes a duty of care to those others – and in converting it to his own use, breaches that duty of care. An example might be a customer who legitimately receives the goods he has ordered – but who then denies having received them, and asks the company to send a replacement item.

This is in contrast to "larceny", when the person originally comes by someone else's property illegally – for example by theft (e.g. walking off with someone else's money without their permission, with the aim of permanently depriving them of that money).

5.5 Investment fraud

Certain frauds involving so-called specialist investment instruments or programmes are relatively specialist – but nonetheless not uncommon. An example perpetrated against the Salvation Army in the 1990s, serves to illustrate the type of investment scam that is common.

Case study: The Salvation Army and a Fraudulent Investment Opportunity

This case dates back to the early 1990s, and fortunately has a relatively happy ending: not all cases end so well.

The Salvation Army had set aside some $10m for possible investment in bank instruments. It had received a proposal that it should invest this money in such instruments as "stand-by letters of credit", having been told that these could be bought and then later sold at potentially significant profit.

It was further told that it could implement this on a repeated basis, so establishing a rolling programme of investments. The proposal was fraudulent.

At the outset, the scam was successful, with nearly $9m being paid away by the Salvation Army. Fortunately, after a lengthy (over 2 years) process of asset tracing and recovery, the money was recovered in full. However the case serves to show that even the largest organisations can fall victim to fraud.

The Salvation Army's recovery of funds was heartening; however a number of useful lessons can be learned from its experience:

- Those responsible for a business' investments should be very cautious of any proposals bearing *any* of the hallmarks of arrangements such as prime bank guarantees, stand-by letters of credit, advance fee arrangements and the like;
- In particular, they should look out for arrangements characterised by references to a "secret" or "confidential" banking market, to which access can – allegedly – only be gained by a favoured few.
- They should not necessarily take comfort from the fact that apparently legitimate advisers such as lawyers/accountants are involved in the process – it is not unknown for such advisers to become embroiled in a scam, whether knowingly or otherwise.

Stand-By Letters of Credit: These are, in fact, perfectly legitimate instruments used in trade finance and as security in a number of situations. They are not, however, used in rolling investment programmes of the type promoted to the Salvation Army.

- They should request full and clear details of the transactions involved, and the parties, and avoid any that involve overly complex or confusing explanations;
- They should be wary of counterparties who appear to prefer to communicate by email or fax, rather than by hard copy and provision of original documents;
- They should exercise particular care of schemes where the sums involved are very substantial: schemes of this nature, in particular, tend to run into tens or hundreds of millions: some have even cited billions of dollars;
- Further, returns are often cited as being of the order of 40–100 per cent per annum;
- Alarm bells should ring if the proposal makes reference to funding from unknown or unconventional lenders, for example foundations or trusts.

A few simple checks can often help avoid disaster. For example, if you suspect that a proposed transaction may be fraudulent:

- Check whether the parties involved are, or should be, regulated in their home or any other jurisdiction;
- Check whether corporate parties to the deal are registered with the appropriate companies registry in their home country (you may be able to do this on-line);
- In particular, verify the loan arranger's corporate details carefully from all available sources;
- Take appropriate references on the parties, from referees whose identity you can also verify;
- For UK counterparties, conduct available credit checks – for example, carry out county court judgement searches for UK companies.

5.6 Third party-against-customer fraud

This type of fraud can most often bedevil financial institutions. Fraudsters may find a variety of innovative ways to claim access to customer's financial accounts, including:

- Simple forgery of a customer request, usually for a payout to a third-party account;
- Forged instructions to change the customer's address, following which the fraudster intercepts mail, assesses the worth of the account and instructs payments or surrenders to himself or other fraudulently established accounts.

The ways in which the fraud or forgery can be initiated also vary: the different types of identity theft discussed in Chapter 2 can enable a fraudster to learn the details of individuals' financial affairs, copy their signatures, learn the personal details which might be used by a financial organisation to verify their identity and even obtain copies of their identity documents.

At the time of writing, a huge number of financial institutions in the UK and offshore British Islands were warned to watch out for a spate of attempted frauds against their own board of directors.

Relying on the expectation that the senior officers of large financial institutions were very likely to have accounts with their own companies, the fraudsters were apparently learning their name and, in some cases, address details by online enquiry of the relevant companies registries and/or telephone directories – and then contacting the institution to request withdrawals. Doubtless they were also relying on the fact that the companies' staff might be unwilling to trouble their bosses with too many tedious identity verification questions over the telephone.

Some simple steps can, however, help to reduce the risk of such frauds. They include things like:

- Customer call-backs (telephone the customer on the last verified number held for him – *not* the one the fraudster might just have advised);
- Flag all accounts held by directors and officers of the company whose details are publicly available, and alert call-centre and administration staff to take extra care with regard to these accounts – both in connection with payment requests, and with requests to change contact details or similar.

5.7 If disaster strikes

As we have noted, once a business has been defrauded in this way, it can be difficult, expensive and often impossible to recover the stolen money. (We will be considering the process of recovery in a later chapter). Professional thieves will launder the stolen funds by quickly cycling it through a number of new structures and countries so as to complicate the audit trail and cause maximum difficulty to the law enforcement authorities.

However, in order to optimise your chances of recovery there are some simple steps you can take:

- If you are to stand any chance of recovering the funds, act promptly and with urgency.
- Once you have established that a fraud has occurred, your first priority should be to freeze all of the fraudster's known assets and accounts with you; this is particularly relevant if your organisation is a financial institution, but can apply in other cases too.
- You will need to involve your lawyers to assist with this as a freezing order from the courts – possibly in a variety of countries – will be necessary. The aim here is to prevent the money from being dissipated before it is too late and there is nothing left to recover.
- Chapter 9, entitled "Immediate Steps", should assist you in the steps to take should a fraud be discovered.

Information, Network
and Internet Security – What
the Non-IT Professional
Needs to Know

The first thing we should agree on is that IT is a powerful tool – it can do great good, transforming the productivity of businesses and facilitating the production of important management information.

It is, however, equally a powerful tool for wrongdoing: money can be transmitted around the world in seconds and once gone, may be difficult or impossible to recover.

Data recovered from electronic devices can prove powerful and robust evidence in cases of suspected fraud, but for this you need a solid understanding of the IT environment, the content and context of the data recovered and the best way to extract and preserve it. In many cases and with expert handling, computers can reveal details which would simply never be obtainable from manual records, even if they were preserved. We will look at some of the key issues, and strategies for dealing with them, in this chapter.

6.1 Assessing the environment – questions your IT expert may ask

Where paper-based records only are involved, many security measures appear commonsensical.

However, many fraud investigators are not computer experts and may therefore be less comfortable that they have taken appropriate steps where the suspected fraud involves the use of office technology. In this case it makes sense to refer to an IT specialist: these are the types of question you may expect him to ask you.

1. **What technological hardware has been in use?**
   - Desktops/laptops/palmtops/mobile phones?
   - Has appropriate password protection been employed? If so what are these?
   - What makes and models of the hardware are involved?
   - What operating systems are in use?
   - Are employees able to use floppy discs/CD ROMs/Pen-drives or similar?
   - For laptops, do they have compatible disc drives available even if there is no integral drive?
   - Does the computer have an internal hard disk drive? Is this partitioned? What is its capacity?
   - What other peripherals does the computer connect to – printers/scanners/fax?

- Are they the property of the company or the employee (or of some other party?)
- Are the computers networked? If so, how? What type of network is involved?
- Where are each relevant user's files stored – on a central network server, or on the user's pc?
- How many network servers are there?
- Can the network be accessed remotely, for example to enable employees to work from home? If so, how is this facilitated?
- Are applications run locally on each affected computer? Do they run on the network itself?
- Where laptops are used to access the network remotely, what applications and areas are accessible?

2. **What software has been available for use?**
   - What applications are available, and are they available to (and used by) all users?
   - Are they proprietary, off the shelf or bespoked applications?
   - In what format, and where, is data saved?
   - Is there evidence of efforts to tamper with data – that is, unusual deletions and/or the use of disc cleaning?

6.2 Securing the technology in a fraud investigation

Where records are kept on computers, the electronic records created can be hugely helpful in the investigation of any suspected frauds. Indeed, they have some considerable advantages over hard copy records:

- Files that have been deleted can generally be recovered, whereas hard copy files, once shredded or burnt may be lost forever.
- Where records have been created, amended or deleted, it is generally possible to identify the time and date of the event – and who carried it out (provided proper use is made of password protection, and similar controls).
- An active policy of taking backups, and testing periodically to ensure that they can be restored, can facilitate the recovery of records and audit trails despite an individual's subsequent deletion of them.

However, despite these strengths, care needs to be taken: if electronically-recorded data is mishandled, it may be destroyed or corrupted: worse, it may lose it value as evidence. Electronic data can be surprisingly fragile, and is vulnerable t corruption – deliberate or otherwise. In addition, there are a number of hard- and software solutions available for "sanitising" equipment (essentially, expunging the data that was previously recorded and making it impossible to recover). Whilst these may be marketed for legitimate purposes – for example, to delete personal information before selling or giving away an old computer, to prevent identity theft and the like – they are also valuable to fraudsters anxious to cover their trail.

It is therefore advisable to take advice from an IT professional before deciding on how to proceed.

The steps you may wish to consider include:

- Identifying an appropriate IT professional to assist in locating and securing the relevant electronic records.
- Assess the IT environment surrounding the data: what access has there been, and is there, to the relevant computer system and terminals?
- How and where will the investigating team be carrying out its job? For example, will it conduct the investigation openly, or will it be taking a low-key or confidential approach? This may depend on:
  - whether the suspect is still working and whether the intention is that he should be aware that he is under investigation or not;
  - whether the company wants the investigation to be generally visible, as a statement that it takes such matters seriously – or whether it wants to keep it confidential so as not to spark concerns as to the sufficiency of its controls. If the latter, more covert, approach is adopted, the team may have to carry out its investigation out of normal working hours;
  - Alternatively, it may be possible to give some alternative explanation for the examination of the hardware – using the pretext of routine maintenance, for example.
- What is the physical security situation – is the relevant hardware in a lockable room and how many people – and who – have access to it?
- Have/should passwords and user access rights been/be revoked or amended?
- Is the system accessible remotely, and if so does this access need terminating or amending?
- Is there any risk of wifi/bluetooth access to the system and does this need terminating?
- Is there any systems-related hardware in the suspect's possession – for example, a laptop at his home, and can this be retrieved (along with any other assets which should be recovered)?

6.3 Capturing the electronic evidence

The investigating team may collect evidence in two ways (and may need to do both):

- Historic – by capturing an image of the evidence already created; and
- Ongoing – by monitoring a suspect's activity on the system

In the former case, where the team wishes to capture records already in existence, it is normal to take a complete "snapshot" of the complete contents of the computer disk, and any other storage medium which might be in use.

Of course, it is important to ensure that the time and date of this snapshot is recorded and that it is retained under secure conditions.

The snapshot, or "source", should in effect be an image of all of:

- The free disk space and any unallocated clusters;
- The directories and folders on the disk;
- The programs used for running applications.

There are a number of different products on the market for making images of disks and other storage media: it is important to select one which is

- Non-invasive (i.e., it will not alter or corrupt the hardware or records it is imaging).
- Of sufficient capacity to hold all the data required. If the investigation requires that an image be taken of one or more file servers, or of a high-capacity disk, then some products will not be able to cope.
- In many cases, sufficiently powerful to make the image quickly. The team may need to give thought to the means of data extraction as this can affect speed: and this may be an issue, especially if the team is constrained in the time available to it – perhaps because it is trying not to advertise the fact that an investigation is underway and is carrying out its activities out of hours.

It is good practice to take at least two images of the data:

1. One for use in the investigation itself (this may be uploaded onto the investigation team's own computer); and
2. One as a permanent, uncorrupted record of the data held on the system as at the date of imaging (a "control" version).

Where the team requires ongoing analysis of systems usage, this may involve products designed for:

- Logging of all keystrokes made on a device or devices;
- Monitoring of network usage to see what sorts of access, and activities, are being undertaken;
- Logging of events at application or system level;
- Utilities which enable the team to view the suspect's screen remotely.

6.4 Examining the images taken

An IT forensics/investigation team may examine computer images using various tools – for example:

- There are tools for this purpose included in many standard suites of utility tools – for example, embedded in the disk imaging package of tools; or
- There are also specific tools which have been created specifically for IT forensic purposes.

As well as reviewing any documents contained in the disk image, the IT forensics team should also look at such things as:

- The internet access log/history;
- Any temporary files;
- Swap space (also known as swap files, or Pagefiles in Windows NT). These are spaces on the hard disk which operate as virtual memory-extensions of the PC's RAM;
- File slack (also known as slack space) – the area between the end of a file, and the end of the cluster in which that file resides. In essence this is wasted storage space, but it is worth examining for the deleted data that may be recoverable from it; and
- Deleted files and fragments of files.

Software also exists that can help the IT forensics team to surmount many hurdles presented by password protection/data encryption.

Depending on the level of sophistication of the fraud, from an IT perspective, the team may also need to have an understanding of newer trends in IT security, encompassing such areas as steganography and cryptography.

Steganography: The practice of putting hidden messages into a document so that its existence is not apparent, in order that only the intended recipient – who knows that it is there – can take steps to read it. An example might be a written message concealed within a communication that to the outside observer looks like a picture.

Cryptography: In contrast, this leaves the existence of the message visible to all but conceals its meaning to those who do not have the "key" to cracking the code or encryption.

It is helpful if, before the IT forensics team begins their work, they can be given some idea of the PC user's level of sophistication and IT literacy; this will help them form a picture of how ingenious, or otherwise, he may have been in concealing his activities and covering his tracks.

6.5 What sorts of information may be recovered? – historic records

Various elements of information may be recovered from a suspect's PC – and this is not limited to the documents that he has generated himself. The potentially valuable data and information which may be recovered includes:

- *Server/PC modem logs.* These can reveal the dates, times and number to which the suspect has dialled from his computer;
- *Fax logs* can similarly yield information on the destination and time of faxes sent; in some cases, faxes sent direct from a desktop computer may also reveal the content of those faxes;
- *Email records* may provide valuable insights into the other parties with whom the suspect has been corresponding, and the content and any attachments may also, of course, prove insightful;
- *Internet cache/history.* This may reveal valuable information as to what web sites/internet sites the individual has visited; this in turn may be instructive in terms of how he has operated the fraud;
- *Personal email accounts* (e.g., web-based arrangement) should be considered as well as the employee's corporate email address;
- *Word-processing packages.* The suspect's PC may hold the footprint of various documents including notes, letters, faxes, memos, invoices, contract

and the like (including documents that have been forged, fabricated or modified on the employer's own system);

- *Spreadsheets/databases.* The PC may hold spreadsheets or databases setting out the programme of fraudulent activity anticipated, or the expected profits therefrom. They may also show that the individual has compiled spreadsheets of the employer's proprietary information, such as price lists, customer lists, sales records and the like;
- *Diary/calendar.* The suspect may have placed meeting reminders, or other notes, as calendar appointments: these can be as useful as the information his e-diary offers about his whereabouts and meeting contacts;
- *Graphics files.* Where a user's PC has been used to download images from the internet (whether offensive or simply unrelated to work) their existence may constitute misuse of the company's PC, and potentially of the employee's paid working hours as well. Whether this falls within the company's definition of a fraud may depend on the individual's terms of employment.
- Before beginning the investigation, the IT forensics team should check the date and time clock of the computer being examined; if this is incorrect, it could lead to incorrect assumptions as to what the suspect did and when.

6.6 What sort of information may be recovered? – ongoing monitoring

In addition to a forensic audit of activities which have taken place on a suspect's computer in the past, the investigation team may wish – whilst the suspect is not aware that he is under suspicion of fraud – to monitor his activities on an ongoing basis.

This involves recording what activities are carried out on a single computer, or indeed on the network, over a given period. It may include:

- Assessing the nature of the access the individual (or individuals) has/have had in the period;
- Viewing activity on a given user's screen remotely;
- Capturing systems and application events through logging, or by recording keystrokes.

Again, there is a variety of tools on the market for these purposes.

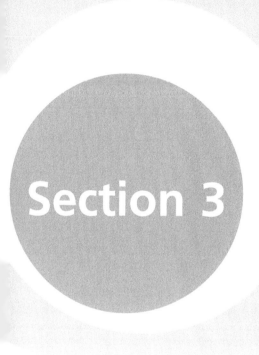

Section 3

Post-event Fraud Management –
What to Do When Your Concerns
Are Aroused That a Fraud Has
Taken Place or Is Being Attempted

The Immediate Steps

7.1   Receipt of a fraud suspicion report

On receipt of a fraud suspicion report, the recipient (i.e. the individual in your organisation identified as being responsible for the receipt of suspicion reports) will need to decide whether or not to instigate an internal investigation.

Generally, an investigation of some sort at least will be made – unless the suspicion report is so clearly unfounded that no useful purpose could possibly be served. In either case the decision, and its rationale, should ideally be documented so that it can be retrieved should the suspicion later prove to have been justified.

A possible format for the recording of fraud suspicion reports, and the decision as to how to proceed is shown in Table 7.1.

It is important that any such decision, and the actions which spin off from it, is taken promptly: especially where the perpetrator is alerted to the fact that he is under suspicion, the first few hours or days can be critical in preserving evidence and securing assets. In particular, any delay or inappropriate first steps may:

- Permit the perpetrator, or those sympathetic to him, to tamper with evidence – thereby covering the tracks of the fraudster;
- Allow the perpetrator to abscond, with or without the assets of which he has defrauded the organisation, and thereby escape justice;
- Allow the assets to be removed or compromised – perhaps, if the perpetrator is alarmed sufficiently to abscond, escalating his activity;
- Complicate or thwart the investigation, adding to costs and time required;
- Render any relevant insurances ineffective.

The purpose of any investigation is to establish the facts in an equitable and objective manner: it is important that the exercise is conducted fairly, having regard for the rights both of the business' stakeholders (including its owners, customers and business partners) and of the suspect.

Thus the investigation should be (and be seen to be) thorough; it should not, however, be carried out in such a way that any suspects are made to feel threatened, or guilty before they are proven to be so. Where criminal offences are suspected, any investigations should – where possible – be carried out to up to a criminal standard of proof.

Table 7.1 Fraud suspicion report log

Fraud Log Ref. No	Date of receipt	Received from	In connection with Account No (if applicable)	Outline OR Location of File with Details	Reported to Law Enforcement (Date, receiving officer)	Action taken re Fraud	Action taken to prevent recurrence
A0001/2007	25 May 2007	John Smith, Accounts Dept	A00001	Request for remittance of funds: client signature does not match	XYZ Crime Unit, officer J Jones	Contact client direct at last confirmed address (letter from CRT, Compliance Officer, 26 May 2007 ref. no ADCV260507). Confirms did not request remittance.	Fraud was avoided this time. However, reinforce staff training on care re client signatures.
Etc.							

7.2   Common first steps

However good your preventative measures, it is – unfortunately – likely that at some point you will be faced with evidence that a fraud has been committed, or at least attempted.

Whatever type of business you are in, the steps you take at this point should be broadly along the following lines (the following are not listed in the order in which they should necessarily be carried out – you will find that many of these activities need to be put in hand immediately, and that several are likely to be underway at the same time);

- Secure the current situation, insofar as is possible – assets, accounts, IT security and the like;
- Ensure that evidence is secured;
- Assemble an investigation team with an appropriate mix of skills;
- Interview relevant witnesses;
- Take control of internal and external communications on the matter, including with law enforcement authorities and regulators;
- Consider whether there are any insurance implications;
- Put in place processes to preserving, trace, locate and recover lost funds/assets;
- Consider and deal with any employment issues;
- Take legal/criminal action against perpetrators where possible and appropriate;
- De-brief at the end of the exercise, so as to benefit from any "lessons to be learnt" – including how systems and controls can be improved to reduce the risk of recurrence.

We have already looked at several of these areas, and will look at others later in the book. Here we will consider those immediate actions not covered elsewhere.

7.3   Securing the evidence

A range of materials may contain data which constitutes relevant "evidence", and so should be secured as quickly as is possible to prevent tampering (or indeed allegations of tampering).

Investigators should consider taking the following steps:

- Secure storage of all relevant items (i.e. in a locked room or cabinet, with appropriate access controls;
- This may include the use of dual controls, for example by the requirement for two keys to access the room;
- Copies should be taken of relevant documents for purposes of the investigation, and to prevent contamination (damage/loss/tampering) to the originals should they be required as evidence in any later criminal prosecution;
- Where this is the case, the documents should be properly organised and referenced, and investigators may wish to consider storing them in evidence bags to prevent contamination;
- Investigators should consider taking electronic copies of (i.e. scanning) relevant documents;
- Referencing – whether of scanned documents or hard copies – should include:
  - The location of the original (e.g. what evidence bag/box it is included in);
  - A unique item reference number;
  - The document type.
- Where scanned copies are used, appropriate backup methods should be used.

The materials which should be considered may include:

- Hard copy (e.g. paper) records;
- Telephone tapes or digital recordings, and logs of telephone usage;
- Electronic documents, including emails, html documents, web interfaces and the like;
- Computer activity logs;
- CCTV footage of activity in the building, if this may indicate access at unusual times or in unauthorised areas;
- In particular, logs relating to the business' security systems, for example in terms of evidencing attempts to circumvent the security system.

The key risk – as soon as the existence of an investigation is out among the staff – is that the perpetrator(s) will take steps to cover their tracks.

In particular, if your are at all concerned that any staff or board members have been involved, it will be a priority to ensure that they cannot impede the investigation or interfere with evidence. This may be very awkward, and you should consider any employment issues when establishing what action to take (see below); but it may be necessary, in order to satisfy regulators, the law enforcement authorities and in due course potentially the public that appropriate precautions have been taken.

You may need to do all of this in a short period of time, and this can strain investigative resources considerably.

Individuals holding relevant documents should be asked to confirm in writing that all relevant documents have been passed to the investigating team. This will help you satisfy the requirements of "discovery" should matters go to court, and you need to demonstrate that you have carried out a positive search for all relevant documents.

Sources of evidence. These may include the records of:

- The individuals involved in the events giving rise to the investigation.
- The compliance department.
- The internal audit department.

The practicalities of securing different types of data. We have already looked at these, but to summarise a few key points:

- *Electronic documents and logs* may be more important than paper records. You may need to act quickly to stop data being inadvertently lost through a routine destruction policy, by being recorded over, or even deliberately tampered with. You should suspend document destruction on all potentially relevant files.
- *Paper documents* which may be relevant should be collected. In some cases, it may be enough to merely request documents from specified individuals. This is fine where the individual is co-operative and understands the scope of the exercise. More often, however, you will need to visit the individuals and departments in question, examine documents in their location and remove all those which could be relevant. In some cases, you will need to do this as a swoop or raid to be sure that all evidence is safe. Archived files may also need to be reviewed.
- *Tapes of telephone calls and telephone logs* should be removed and analysed. Telephone logs may also contain useful information.
- *Security system logs* may be reviewed to see who had physical access to specific areas at a particular time.

Document handling. You should ensure that the team follows some standard procedures when collecting and handling data:

- *Evidence bags.* Ensure that they record the exact location from which each document was collected, and from whose control or possession it was taken. One practical way to record this information is to use a separate evidence bag for each location from which documents are collected. Here, the term "location" can be taken to mean an entire room – or, depending on volume, to the contents of a particular filing cabinet. Each evidence bag so created should have a unique reference number, and the relevant information enclosed, noted on it.

- *Document management systems.* Ideally, and especially where the volume of records is sizeable, all paper documents seized should be scanned into a computer (preferably one which is dedicated to the project and to which access is closely controlled). All relevant information, including evidence bag numbers, the document reference numbers, and objective and subjective codings should be recorded against the document's image.
- Each document should be allocated a unique document reference number, which will be used to identify it in the future – and to allow efficient recovery of the original document. The reference number should be cross referenced to the number of the evidence bag in which the document was collected, so that it is possible to determine the exact location of that document at the time it was seized. This can be important if the documents are relied on in any subsequent criminal or regulatory action.
- Documents should also be given objective and subjective codes:
  - The "objective code" gives details such as the document's date, its author, the intended recipient and the document type.
  - The "subjective code" tells the team what area of the investigation the document seems to relate to.

If you have many documents to deal with, it may be worth investing in specialist software to deal with these aspects.

It is advisable to make an electronic copy of all scanned documents, which can be used as a working copy.

- *Storage.* You will need to ensure that the documents the team is working with can be stored securely. This may require the provision of a separate "case room" where all investigation documents are stored – and perhaps, where the majority of work can be done, outside the view of the main workforce.

  Access to this room should of course be carefully restricted to protect the evidential value of the documents. If employees need to access the documents for their day-to-day work, they should be given photocopies only so as to preserve the originals for any litigation or prosecution which ensues. You should maintain a register of:

- each document stored in the case room;
- when, and by whom (and why), documents are removed and returned;
- when, and to whom (and why), photocopies are passed to employees.

The following brief checklist may act as an *aide memoire:*

Checklist: Preserving the evidence

You should ensure you consider all of the following:

- Electronic documents and logs;
- Paper documents;
- Tapes of telephone calls and telephone logs;
- CCTV of the premises;
- Security system logs.

The following procedures may be required:

- Use of evidence bags;
- Scanning of all paper documents;
- Record the following against each scanned image:
  - evidence bag number;
  - a unique document reference number;
  - an objective code;
  - a subjective code.
- Make a working copy of each scanned document;
- Store evidence in a secure case room;
- Restrict access to the case room;
- Control and record to whom copies of seized documents are released.

.4 Assembling the investigation team

One of your first aims should be to ensure that where necessary, any decisions can be made *quickly* by someone who has the appropriate level of authority, and who is not compromised by being involved in the problem.

Because it can be hard to identify senior individuals who have not been involved with the issue itself, it may make sense to appoint a non-executive member of the board (e.g. a member of the audit committee, if there is one, or the non-executive chairman).

This individual should then prepare an action plan and, if the scale of events warrants it, call a board meeting to approve it.

Whilst a non-executive appointment may be important for the avoidance of conflicts, and to ensure an independent investigation, you may however also need to appoint a senior executive to the team as well – so as to deal with the practical issues that the investigation team will need to address. An example of this may be where the investigators need the co-operation of employees within the company. Unless the non-executive's plan is supported or implemented by an individual perceived by the workforce as having real, day-to-day authority, the investigators may find the staff generally unwilling to assist in tasks outside the normal scope of their jobs.

A key priority for the individual or individuals leading the investigation will then be to determine who the investigation team should comprise. This will involve a consideration of:

- the resources required (how many people are needed to review the volume and type of documents involved, and to carry out the other elements of the investigation?);
- what general skills will they need (e.g. will the disciplines of the internal audit team be appropriate to carry on the investigation?);
- what specialist skills will be required (e.g. will an IT forensic specialist be required, or someone with knowledge of the financial markets?);
- generally, a member of the legal team should be involved – both to provide legal advice on a range of matters (see later in this chapter) and, where possible and appropriate, to ensure that privilege is secured for as many documents as is possible;
- where individuals from the operational side of the business are needed, who is least likely to be compromised (for example through responsibility for a department or function which may have been the subject of the abuse);
- how will the business carry on with "business as usual" where key individuals are diverted to support the investigation?

Team briefing

Once the team has been assembled, there should be a prompt and detailed briefing meeting. The agenda should include:

- An outline of the concerns;
- A briefing on any technical aspects of the case (for example, some guidance on accounting rules if the issue at hand relates to balance sheet fraud; a description of the product and the appropriate way of dealing with it, if the fraud relates to the mis-pricing of a derivative financial instrument in a collective investment scheme);
- Circulation of any materials the team is to review immediately;
- An overview of the investigation action plan and work programme;
- Specific instructions to individual team members;
- Any steps that need to be taken when drafting new documents to preserve privilege (for more on this, see Chapter 11);
- A briefing on the need for confidentiality, subject to any obligations the business may be under to make appropriate disclosures to regulators, insurers, law enforcement authorities.

Communication between team members and so on

In order for the investigation to be as thorough and quick as possible, clear and effective communication between the members of the team is critical. This is considerably aided by a clear and detailed programme of work.

Subject to issues of privilege (see later and Chapter 11), the plan should be maintained in a single document, which is regularly updated and circulated to key individuals.

It may be appropriate – again subject to careful controls to preserve confidentiality and privilege – for members of the team to keep each other up to date by circulating a daily float file, holding copies of all documents generated by them. The team should meet regularly, possibly as small sub-groups, so as to report on progress and consider the next stages of their activities.

.5   Overseeing external communications

For public companies listed on a stockmarket, it may be necessary to make an announcement to avoid the creation of a false market in those shares. (Indeed, in very extreme cases, shares in the company may need to be suspended from trading).

This is an area where a decision should be taken promptly, if need be with the benefit of legal advice. That said, however, and whilst failure to act appropriately could result in regulatory, civil or even criminal action, it could be equally damaging to over-react from a lack of forethought – forming ill-founded gut reactions and passing them on to the market. (Indeed to do so could be as misleading as to have said nothing at all).

For this reason, you should ensure that as much has been done as possible to establish the scale and nature of the problem *before* you make any announcement – and at the time, you should ideally be in a position to comment on any terminations or suspensions of senior individuals' employments – and the company's strategy for the future.

Depending on the nature of the organisation, you may also be required to make certain disclosures in the context of an existing transaction, or a transaction the company is about to enter into – for example, relating to the fitness or propriety of its management.

You may well also need, on an ongoing basis, to keep a range of bodies briefed as to progress. These may include:

- Regulators;
- The police;
- Banks;
- The media.

We will look at dealings with external parties in Chapter 9.

7.6 Legal issues on an investigation

As we have already noted, a member of the legal department (or perhaps the company's external lawyers) should generally be on the investigation team. In any event where necessary, their advice should be sought on:

- The structure of the investigation;
- Issues such as confidentiality and privilege;
- The proper conduct of the investigation;
- The collection of evidence and interviewing of witnesses;
- Employee issues, especially where suspension or termination of employment are concerned;
- Investigations by, and interactions with, regulators and the police;

- The company's, and its officers', potential liabilities;
- Any claims against third parties which the company may have.

7.7 Preserving, tracing and recovering lost assets

Once it is clear that a fraud has been perpetrated or attempted, you should take steps to:

- Prevent any assets from being lost (or prevent the loss of more assets);
- Begin the process of tracing and recovering those that *have* been lost.

Preventing further loss

If you know who the perpetrator of the fraud is, then:

- Curtail the individual(s) authority and permissions to move or withdraw funds/assets, to execute contracts on the company's behalf, or carry out any other sensitive activities;
- Inform your bank, other holders of your company's assets (and, in appropriate cases, the company's customers and counterparties) that this is the case (NB: you should however exercise care in giving reasons for the curtailment of the individual's authorities. In some cases it may be best to give no reason at all until the situation is absolutely clear. You may need to take legal advice);
- Suspend the individual's access to the company's computer system and records;
- Where appropriate, change passwords, security codes and locks;
- If physical measures such as changing security passes will take time, you may need to use security staff to stop the suspect gaining access to files, computers or the premises as a whole;
- Consider obtaining injunctive relief to freeze the suspect's assets.

If you do not know the perpetrator's identity, then you should interview suspects as soon as possible (we will look at this in greater depth in the next chapter). Until you are more certain of who is involved, it may be appropriate to adopt a more cautious approach.

This is because there is, of course, the risk of alerting the suspect and allowing him to abscond or remove more assets. From some perspectives it may seem wisest to withdraw authorities/deny access to a larger number of people; however, the company still needs to operate and you will need to balance this against the risk of operational issues – and possibly also of damaging relationships with a number of innocent staff.

Tracing lost assets

To the extent that assets have already been lost, you should initiate steps to trace and recover them. Here, more than almost anywhere else, it is essential to act quickly.

Rather than confronting the individual or calling the police, your legal department may suggest that a first step should be to:

- obtain an injunction to attach (or freeze) the suspect's assets – wherever they are –; and
- to try and find out where he has hidden the rest by simultaneously obtaining disclosure orders.

Promptness, and the element of surprise, are the essential elements in applications for injunctions and attachment orders to recover lost assets. However you should weigh the need for speed against any legal obligations you have for proper disclosure or investigation. You should therefore have investigated as fully as possible in the time frames allowed before making an application – there is no point in being granted an injunction quickly if it is subsequently discharged. We will look further at some of these issues in the next chapter.

Investigation Techniques
and Next Steps

8.1 Interviewing witnesses

As part of your investigation, and unless you are in the very early stages and attempting not to let suspects know that their fraud has been discovered, you are very likely to need to interview certain employees.

You may well need to involve your in-house or external lawyers in this process. In England and Wales, employees are contractually obliged to obey reasonable instructions from their employers, and this would include:

- reasonable attendance at interviews (i.e. during working hours, under reasonable conditions and not in the middle of the night!); and
- the provision of accurate and complete information during the course of an investigation.

Where an employee fails to co-operate with an investigation, this is likely to be an act of misconduct for which he could be disciplined. We will look at employment issues a little later.

The two main issues for an employer to consider are

- the conduct of the interview; and
- whether the employee should have separate representation.

An interviewer should aim to use "open" questions, so as to elicit the maximum amount of information. Judgemental questioning or comments should be avoided, so as not to antagonise or unnecessarily alarm the interviewee.

A basic framework for the interview can be useful: but a good interviewer will be flexible enough to respond to an unexpected direction in responses, and adapt accordingly.

You may find that an initially uncooperative interviewee can be prompted into answering questions on production of documents which involve him in some way – for example, having been signed or initialled by him.

The interviewer will need to assess whether the interviewee is being truthful. Here, body language and demeanour can be useful to those skilled in such matters; otherwise, the best method may be to assess his responses against known facts.

8.2 How to carry on the interview

Your company's disciplinary procedure (which should be set out in the Staff Handbook) may well establish the guidelines for conducting interviews with staff in the context of investigations into wrongdoing. These should be followed closely unless there are exceptional circumstances, and in those cases you should take legal advice.

One of the first questions to consider is – who should conduct the interviews? This should be considered in light of various issues, including:

- The independence of the questioner;
- Whether the questioner (or indeed anyone else present at the interview) might inhibit the witness from giving frank answers.

In many cases, external parties such as the company's lawyer or auditor may be appropriate, since they should have the requisite independence. They may well also be skilled in this type of investigative questioning. Their presence may, however, be quite intimidating – especially to more junior staff.

It is essential that the interviewee is forwarned that the interview should be treated confidentially, so as to prevent them from discussing it with their colleagues and perhaps undermining the investigation, or starting damaging leaks to the outside world.

You should also consider how best to record the interview. Options include:

- Tape recording;
- Having an independent transcript writer (but these two first options can again be quite formal and intimidating);
- Alternatively, you could consider having an additional attendee at the interview whose main role is to take notes – but who minimises the intrusiveness of this by participating in the interview itself. This may be because of their relevant knowledge of the issues, and this individual may be able to ask pertinent questions which the main interviewer might have overlooked.

You will also need to consider the structure of the interview.

- Will one suffice?
- Or is it likely that one or more subsequent interviews will be required to follow up on issues as they are investigated?

The interviewer should prepare thoroughly, by considering all the issues that should be raised – and the best order for them. If the interviewer is an external party such as a lawyer, he should prepare his questions in discussion with someone with the requisite operational knowledge to prompt him appropriately. In general, it is useful to begin with broad questions on each area, drilling down to more specific key points as required.

It may be appropriate to ask the interviewee to read and sign a copy of the interview notes or transcript, or a statement recording his opinion. This limits his scope for later retractions, and may focus his thoughts and elicit further information. If he will not agree to read and sign such a document, this lack of co-operation may amount to misconduct.

8.3 Separate representation

You should consider whether the employee being interviewed should be offered the option to be accompanied by a representative of his choice. (Again there may be guidance in the Staff Handbook). Such a representative could be:

- a colleague or friend (usually only appropriate for disciplinary proceedings); or
- a legal representative, so as to avoid any problems with the interview being construed as "oppressive" – this could render any evidence so obtained as inadmissible in the event of criminal proceedings.

There are pluses and minuses to both options, and you should take legal advice if in any doubt:

- On the one hand, it seems fair to tell your employees that they are entitled to (and it may be in their interests to) have legal representation;
- On the other, if the enquiry is at that stage still purely internal, there is nothing that should prevent an employer from questioning its own employees, fully and properly recorded, so as to find out what it can about its own affairs. Arguably, the company's senior staff and officers have a duty to do all they can, and as quickly as they can, to protect their employer's interests – regardless of any sensitivities towards the potentially fraudulent employee.

sensible approach seems to be this: with a view to not alarming your witnesses – hether they are suspects or otherwise – and so as not to discourage them from co-operating with you, consider *not* suggesting that they seek separate represen-tation *unless and until there is good cause* – but at that stage, *ensure that you do so, promptly.*

This means that whilst you are still in the early stages of what is as yet a purely internal investigation, you may not need to do so. You are simply undertaking a fact-finding exercise. If the employee himself requests legal representation, he should not as a general rule be denied it; but it should not usually be necessary to suggest he seeks it before a first interview.

If and when it becomes apparent that an external investigation of some kind may be needed, either against the company itself or against staff or other individuals associated with it, then – even if this is at a very early point in your enquiries – the whole issue of legal representation for witnesses becomes instantly more sensitive.

If, for example, it seems as if the interests of a witness could differ from those of the company (perhaps because he is implicated in some wrongdoing and your company anticipates that it will have to disclose his activities to an outside investi-gatory body), then you should normally advise him to seek separate representation. You should, generally, do this as soon as the issue becomes apparent.

Do not suggest that the interviewee asks for advice from the company's own lawyers or in-house legal department. If you do so, and the company's interests and his diverge, then the adviser may find he has a conflict of interests and may no longer be able to act for either of you.

8.4 Considering employment issues

Where documents, interviews or events indicate that employees or officers of the company have participated in an attempted or actual fraud, you will need to decide from an employment perspective how to deal with them. As well as taking appropriate legal advice, you should involve your company's Human Resources department to ensure that any internal guidelines are adhered to.

Among the legal issues you will need to consider are

- Employment legislation;
- The European Convention on Human Rights, in terms of how the employee is treated;

- The Data protection Act 1998, in terms of how information relating to the case and to the employee's conduct is handled (including in the event of subsequent requests for references, from future prospective employers);
- The legislation on your rights as an employer to monitor employee communications and so on.

You may need to consider disciplinary action, suspension or even termination of an employee's job. As well as the legislation, you should take account of relevant provisions in his contract of employment, and the company's procedures.

8.5 Post-investigation de-briefing

In most cases of fraud or attempted fraud, there will be useful lessons to be learned by the company (even if these are no more than "we have perfectly good procedures and controls in place – we need to improve training and awareness so that *people follow them!*").

In addition, some form of post-investigation review may be required by internal or outside parties, such as:

- the company's regulator, if it has one;
- its auditors;
- its bank;
- its loss insurers;
- its board of directors or Audit Committee.

All of these parties will be keen for you to satisfy them that the company's exposure to fraud in the future has been minimised.

A review of this nature can take a variety of forms, from a complete systems audit to a simple meeting of relevant managers, depending on the case.

Investigation checklist: Immediate priorities

- Securing the assets;
- Prevention of further fraud; curtail authorisations and begin interviews of employees suspected of involvement immediately;
- Secure the evidence, both for the investigation and for possible civil/criminal proceedings;

- Consider any solvency implications for the company;
- Consider directors' duties;
- Make any necessary notifications (regulators/insurers may have to be notified immediately on discovery, or indeed immediately concerns become real suspicions);
- Plan PR for quality and consistency of message – both internal (staff) and external (press, customers);
- Begin asset recovery as soon as possible;
- Make investigation resource available – team, investigation and interview rooms, computer as scanned document database.

Longer-term priorities

Seek to establish:

- Exactly how much has been lost;
- If and how controls were circumvented;
- How the fraud came to light;
- What should be done to prevent recurrence.

8.6   Securing the assets

We have mentioned the need to secure the company's assets a number of times the aim here is to prevent the risk of further loss.

If you know who has been involved, and company employees are included, the first step is to remove their authority to move or withdraw funds or other assets - or to execute contracts – immediately. You will need to inform external parties such as banks, and perhaps also suppliers and customers.

You may wish to remove the individual from his position of authority, and prevent him accessing his office and/or computer files.

You should immediately secure his files – documents and computer records – and prevent him from removing anything from the building (including even personal diaries and handwritten notes, as these can – as we shall see – contain important evidence).

The individual should also have his user rights suspended from the company's computer system as a whole (including any remote access via a modem link). Passwords, security codes and physical locks should be changed. You should also ensure that computer back-ups are taken promptly.

8.7 Prevention of further fraud

In terms of preventing further frauds – either an escalation of the one under investigation or new events – you should consider interviewing all suspected staff as promptly as possible after discovery of the fraud.

You may only have one chance to have a truly effective interview; therefore, as we have already seen, it is important that the right interviewer is selected and that he is properly informed. Your company's disciplinary rules should be followed consistently.

As we have already noted, it may be necessary to suspend or terminate an individual's employment; and we have seen that it is important to observe the applicable legislation, the terms of his contract, and the company's own disciplinary rules. In any event it will usually be reasonable to suspend an individual (albeit perhaps on full pay) if the investigation involves gross misconduct.

Before taking such action, the employee should be given an opportunity to respond to any allegations – and to have any mitigating factors taken into consideration.

Other steps include physical ones such as:

- changing computer passwords;
- changing locks;
- retrieving office keys;
- amending security codes and bank authorisations;
- prohibiting certain personnel from specific areas of the building.

8.8 Directors' duties and solvency

the fraud is, or appears that it may be, sufficiently sizeable it may threaten the solvency of the company as a whole (consider the case of Barings if you doubt this). For this reason, it is important that – especially in the case of significant frauds – the directors are apprised of events so that they can consider their obligations.

If they know, or ought to conclude, that there is no real prospect of the company doing anything other than going into an insolvent liquidation then they have a duty to take action to minimise the creditors' potential losses. Failure to do so may leave them liable to contribute personally (on account of "wrongful trading"), in an amount calculated to reflect the loss attributable to their acts or failure to act.

Directors who fail to act promptly and appropriately face additional risks to the one of wrongful trading highlighted above; they may also be:

- disqualified under the relevant companies acts provisions; and
- in those jurisdictions where acting as a director by way of business is a licensable activity (for example the Isle of Man), may also lose their licensed status and face other regulatory sanctions.

Thus it is important that members of the board ensure, on an ongoing basis, that they receive and consider adequate information about the company's affairs (both financial and otherwise) – so that they can take prompt steps if insolvent liquidation becomes a prospect.

As soon as a director becomes aware of such an issue (or has concerns that it may be the case) he should therefore raise the matter with his colleagues on the board so as to enable them to take professional advice, if need be. For this reason the director overseeing the investigation should keep his colleagues briefed approximately on the progress. If there is any doubt, the company should ensure that it stops incurring any further debts immediately, pending receipt of this advice.

In cases like this, directors are obliged to take all steps available to them to minimise creditors' losses. If they conclude that the company cannot continue to trade, they must instigate appropriate procedures.

Where one director is more pessimistic about the future than the others, and cannot persuade them of his view, he may feel he is in a difficult position; it may be in order for him to resign his board appointment but he would be well advised to take personal independent advice before doing so, to ensure that he has no omitted any actions he could have taken to protect the company's creditors. In such a case, of course, there will be an increased onus on the remainder of the board.

More generally, of course, directors are required to act with skill consistent with their personal qualifications (including in connection with suspected or actual frauds). Nonetheless, if in doubt they should obtain independent legal advice.

8.9 Recovery of funds

Where assets have been lost, you will need to consider certain legal and practical/commercial issues in deciding on how to act. Points to consider include:

- How much has been lost, and whether it is worth going to expense to recover it;
- How much any litigation may cost (this can be hard to estimate);
- How complex the related legal issues are;
- What the likelihood of success is;
- Whether any insurances will cover the loss, and what the insurers' view is. In some cases, insurers will insist on taking over the handling of the case and any associated litigation;
- If the assets have been transferred abroad, where any proceedings should be instigated;
- What the relevant local legal system is like, and whether this may favour the fraudster;
- Can the transfer itself be attacked (you, or your company's lawyers, may need to engage local legal advisers to advise on such matters as what freezing orders or similar may be secured through the local courts).

Where assets have been transferred overseas, matters can become complicated and are not always favourable to the original true owner:

- You may need to provide evidence that the assets are traceable – that is, your company is indeed the true beneficial owner of the assets;
- Or, you may need to provide evidence to support an attachment of the assets – for example, proof that the local party who now ostensibly owns them did in fact defraud the company, and should now compensate the company as a debtor;
- You may have to obtain court orders not only in the country to which you have traced the assets, but also in other countries through which they have passed.
- It may be simpler to try and persuade the local law enforcement authorities to commence a criminal prosecution, supported by appropriate freezing orders. In some cases, the defrauded company may then be able to join in the action as a *partie civile* – with a view to obtaining redress from the frozen assets. This can be a cheaper option than the purely civil route discussed above. You should take advice on the most appropriate option in the relevant country.

- A further option can be to try and put the fraudster's companies into liquidation. This can provide useful tools to attack his arrangements (for example, an English liquidator has powers to require third parties to provide information and answer questions). There are, however, a number of counterbalancing disadvantages to this approach; for example, the loss of control, an additional layer of costs, and competition for the distributed assets from other creditors.

The most important factor in any successful recovery of assets is being able to freeze them as quickly as is possible: otherwise they can be routed through a variety of countries, currencies and structures with frightening speed. Every jurisdiction through which the funds pass adds another layer of cost and complexity, and makes the chances of a successful location and recovery more remote.

You should consider engaging professional help in tracing the assets which have been defrauded – far better to rely on specialists who are well versed in the procedures – although you may manage to find some information yourselves through such means as:

- Company searches;
- Searches of registers of company officers and directors;
- Regulatory databases;
- Land and property registry searches;
- Scanning of media output;
- Dun & Bradstreet, and similar.

A detailed discussion of the various types of order, injunction and other mechanism (including discovery) is outside the scope of this text. However, the following are just some of the elements of English law which may assist in tracking, and ultimately in recovering, assets.

- *Mareva injunctions* derive their name from a case known as *Mareva Compania Naviera SA* v. *International Bulk Carriers (SA [1975], 2 Lloyds Report* 509). They act to preserve assets held by someone, to support a claim against him in connection with, for example, a fraud. He will be prevented from removing assets from the country, or otherwise dealing with them. In some limited cases (*Derby* v. *Weldon (Nos 3&4) [1989] 2WLR* 412) the injunction may have effect on assets held outside the country. The assets will only be released to the victim once it has obtained final judgment. The cour will require three conditions to be met before granting a Mareva injunction. They are:

- That there is a good claim on the assets;
- That there are assets within the jurisdiction (except in the limited cases where for example a worldwide Mareva injunction is granted); and
- There is a real risk that the fraudster will dissipate them so as to defeat any later judgment.

So that the injunction will have the benefit of surprise, the order is obtained without notice to the fraudster; but it is common to co-ordinate the application with notice to relevant banks and similar, so as to speed up the process once the order has been obtained.

- *Tracing injunctions* are aimed at freezing the specific property which has been misappropriated (or the proceeds of that property) – unlike a Mareva, which freezes any of the fraudster's own assets regardless of whether they are the same ones he misappropriated from the company. The procedure, however, is broadly the same. To successfully obtain a tracing injunction, you must prove an "arguable" case for a claim – a test which is somewhat less demanding than that for a Mareva.

- *Disclosure Orders.* Those who are (albeit unwittingly) "mixed up" in fraud, even though not a party to the action are likely to come under a duty to assist the defrauded party – providing information on, for example, what they know of the whereabouts and extent of the fraudster's assets. Examples of disclosure orders to support this include those known as *Norwich Pharma* orders – again the name derives from a past case.

- *Anton Piller orders.* These can enable the victim of a fraud to search for, and seize, relevant documents from the fraudster; this may help them track down the funds that have gone missing.

We have not touched on the wide range of powers available to the law enforcement authorities under various statutes – for example, under the Proceeds of Crime Act and similar; however these may well also be valuable tools should they be involved in the pursuit of the assets.

Dealing with External Parties: Regulators, Insurers and the Law Enforcement Authorities

9.1 General

We have touched briefly on the need for care in communications. In the next chapter we will consider the legal issues associated with this (that is, the need to preserve legal privilege and similar wherever possible). Here we will consider some wider issues relating to dealings with the outside world in the aftermath of a fraud.

9.2 Dealing with regulators

The situation here will depend on whether the company itself is subject to regulation – either in its home country, or in other countries in which it is active. For example, businesses engaging in banking or most other financial services activities will be regulated by the Financial Services Authority; those in the provision of legal advice, by the Law Society.

In many cases, regulators have powers enabling them to investigate the activities of their members/licenceholders, and often of the individuals associated with them. Companies within their remit may be subject to rules or codes of conduct which set out when they must report a suspected fraud to their regulator.

If you are responsible for overseeing fraud investigations and similar, you should ensure that you are familiar with your business' reporting obligations to any relevant regulators; your compliance department, or failing that your in-house or external legal advisers should be able to assist you with this.

They should also be able to provide advice on the appropriateness – or otherwise – of providing the regulators with any witness statements and similar that you may gather. (For more on this see Chapter 11.)

Bear in mind that in the event of a disclosure to your regulator, that regulator may be interested in much more than the immediate facts of the case. It may, for example:

- be concerned over any indications that your company has poor systems and controls, or that there are other factors which predispose it to fraudulent abuse;
- have concerns for the company's solvency;
- wish to satisfy itself that customers' interests are not at risk;

- wish to take enforcement action against the company or its personnel if there is evidence of wrongdoing – or indeed in some cases of negligence or incompetence.

Generally speaking, of course, a responsible organisation will wish to cooperate with any enquiries or investigations being made by its industry regulator – not least because failure to do so may result in disciplinary action against it (and at worst, loss of its license to operate).

However there are some circumstances in which it may be wise to take advice before disclosing all documents unquestioningly (see Chapter 11) – and indeed to ensure that you have properly established the regulator's powers and remit before complying (see Chapter 11).

The exact reactions of a company's regulator will depend on the nature of the regulated industry it is engaged in, the regulator's powers and the degree of "invasiveness" with which the regulator carries out its duties (some regulators are relatively light in their touch, whilst others can become heavily involved in a company's day-to-day affairs).

In any event, the following issues may be considered by it in determining what – if any – regulatory intervention to undertake:

- *Impact on the company's financial standing.* In most industries – and in particular in the field of financial services – the regulator will be keen to understand whether the fraud has the potential to undermine the company's ability to carry on as a going concern;
- *Corporate governance implications.* The regulator may be keen to determine whether there were failings in the company's systems and controls, and whether any of its corporate officers or staff are implicated;
- *Impact on customers, investors and other counterparties.* Regulatory intervention may be influenced by the degree to which the interests of customers investors and indeed other groups (for example former employees of the company who are now drawing pensions from its occupational scheme) have been put at risk;
- *Open-ness in dealing with the regulator.* If any regulatory enforcement action is envisaged (for example, a fine on the company or its individual officer for failure to implement proper systems and controls to limit the risk of fraud), then the scale of this enforcement action may be mitigated by the promptitude and frankness with which the company alerts its regulator.

- *Compliance with applicable codes, regulations and the like.* In some industries, the regulator oversees specific legislation, codes and – in some cases – voluntary guidelines. It is likely to consider the extent to which the company has complied with these, when determining what action to take.

The following case illustrates the type of regulatory action that may be taken by an industry regulator – in this case the Financial Services Authority – where a company is a victim of a fraud but is deemed to have taken insufficient steps to protect itself from abuse.

FSA fines BNPP Private Bank £350,000 for weak anti-fraud controls

Press release 10 May 2007: "The Financial Services Authority (FSA) has today fined BNP Paribas Private Bank (BNPP Private Bank) £350,000 for weaknesses in its systems and controls which allowed a senior employee to fraudulently transfer £1.4 million out of clients' accounts without permission.

This is the first time a private bank has been fined for weaknesses in its anti-fraud systems. The 13 fraudulent transactions were carried out between February 2002 and March 2005 using forged clients' signatures and instructions and by falsifying change of address documents.

During its investigation, the FSA found that BNPP Private Bank did not have an effective review process for large transactions, over £10,000, from clients' accounts. It also found that the bank's procedures were not clear about the role of senior management in checking significant transfers prior to payment. As a result, a number of fraudulent transactions were not independently checked. In addition, a flaw in the bank's IT system allowed the senior employee to evade the normal Middle Office processes. This meant that basic authorisation and signatory checks were not carried out on internal cash transfers between different customer accounts.

Margaret Cole, FSA Director of Enforcement, said: "BNPP Private Bank's failures exposed clients' accounts to the risk of fraud. This is unacceptable particularly with the overall increase in awareness around fraud and client money risks. Senior management must make sure their firms have robust systems and controls to reduce the risk of them being used to commit financial crime.

"This is a warning to other firms that we are raising our game in this area and expect them to follow suit. We will not hesitate to take action against any firm found wanting."

BNPP Private Bank's failings were serious because they enabled significant fraud to take place and failed to detect subsequent transfers to cover it up for a long period of time. The bank also failed to improve its procedures for monitoring large transactions or carry out remedial action on a timely basis. This was despite the bank being aware that certain of its procedures required improvement as a result of an FSA visit in relation to money laundering systems and controls in August 2002 and subsequent internal reviews.

The FSA recognises that BNPP Private Bank has since taken steps to correct the failings and no customers suffered loss. Also, a subsequent independent review of the bank's anti-fraud systems and controls found them to have no significant weaknesses. The bank brought the fraud to the FSA's attention and has co-operated fully with the investigation. BNPP Private Bank qualified for a 30 % discount under the FSA's executive settlement procedures by agreeing to settle at an early stage of the investigation.

In the last two years, the FSA has fined Nationwide, Capita Group and Kyte for weaknesses in their anti fraud systems and controls."

Source: http://www.fsa.gov.uk/pages/Library/Communication/PR/2007/060.shtml

A regulator may also expect (and may have powers to insist upon) close involvement in the ongoing investigation.

Many regulators will expect that their licensed/authorised companies will bring potential fraud issues to their attention promptly upon discovery – indeed this may be a regulatory requirement and failure to do so may be a breach of regulations or the law. The organisation should weigh up, and if need be take advice on, the benefits of prompt notification, against the risks and disadvantages of notifying a regulator of something which on fuller investigation proves to have been unwarranted.

In most cases, as well as the immediate impact, the regulator will take a close interest in other areas of the investigation. Even where the investigation itself is being carried out efficiently and all appropriate steps are being taken, the public and accountable nature of a regulator's duties may place an onus on it to be seen to take action – which may include disciplinary action against the company and/or its officers (for example, the FSA has a noted track record of fining and "naming and shaming" miscreants in the financial services industry, as is seen in the BNPP case study set out earlier).

In any event, if the fraud has been facilitated through weak systems, controls or culture, the regulator is likely to insist on an action plan to remedy the areas of weakness, and to prevent a recurrence; and will be likely to monitor and follow-up on the implementation of this action plan.

9.3 Dealing with the Police/other Law Enforcement Authorities

In some cases, you may have no choice as to whether to involve the police or prosecuting authorities; a regulatory investigation may, for example, reveal matters which bring about criminal investigation of individuals or the company itself.

In other cases, however, there may not be such a requirement and you may feel that your company's interests can best be protected through appropriate civil action. Criminal prosecutions can damage a company's reputation, because of the publicity that tends to flow from them.

Once a fraud is referred to the law enforcement authorities, the company is likely to lose control over whether it goes forward to a prosecution. The law enforcement authorities will expect – and can often require – co-operation from the company, and this can result in costly and time-consuming disruption to "business as usual".

A deciding factor may be whether disclosure to the police would prevent third parties from being damaged by the fraudster.

In addition, of course, the involvement of the law enforcement authorities may actually assist the company in recovering its assets – a big consideration, in size-able frauds, and one which may outweigh any reputational negatives that ensue.

- In some countries, the types of asset freezing and asset recovery orders discussed in the previous chapter are more readily available to the police than to a civil law claimant;

- In contrast to the powers of your internal investigation team, the police may be able to search the suspects' homes for evidence (and indeed it may be important – from a relationship and reputational perspective – that any such searches are carried out under the auspices of authorities other than the company);
- If you plan to claim from your insurers – for example, under an employee fidelity policy – it may be a requirement of the policy that the matter is referred to the police.

You should remember that there are some cases where reporting to the authorities (in this case, the Serious and Organised Crime Authority or "SOCA") is mandatory – for example, in the case of those working for regulated financial services businesses who become aware of, or suspicious that there is, money laundering or terrorist financing activity.

Some companies have an internal policy of reporting crimes – fraudulent and otherwise – as a matter of course, no matter what the disruption caused and regardless of whether there is any economic benefit in doing so. This may be because:

- Articulating such a policy sends a clear message to employees and outsiders alike that offenders will be prosecuted – thereby acting as a deterrent to those contemplating fraud; or
- Because it is seen as the "right thing to do" and the company is keen to be seen to act responsibly in the interests of society as a whole.

9.4   Dealing with the company's bankers

The company's bank may be involved in the investigation for a variety of reasons

- because money held with it is the subject of a freezing injunction;
- because its personnel are required to give witness statements or otherwise assist with the investigation; or
- in the worst-case scenario, because the company's financial situation has been damaged by the fraud.

In the latter case, the bank may need to be persuaded to continue supporting the company – perhaps by extending overdraft facilities or otherwise providing credit. If there is an issue with the company's solvency, then it is not unusual for a bank to insist on a high degree of involvement in the overall handling of the fraud investigation and pursuit of assets.

9.5   Dealing with the company's insurers

In the event that your company falls victim to a fraud, you should ensure that you do not overlook the possible insurance implications:

- on the one hand, there may well be insurances which can help to cover some of the costs or losses you incur;
- on the other, failure to notify your insurers promptly of the loss event may mean that the policy will not pay out on the fraud related claim – or indeed, perhaps, in connection with other subsequent claims, if it is a condition of the policy that you will inform them promptly of such events.

Company insurance policies may cover the following:

- Under the Directors & Officers' ("D&O") policy, the company may be able to reclaim expenses incurred by members of the board who liase with the law enforcement authorities;
- Under an Employee Fidelity Policy (and frequently other types of policy), sums misappropriated and the costs of recovering them may be covered.

The fraud risk manager should ensure that he is familiar with the relevant terms of the company's insurance policy, including any notification requirements and deadlines – failure to comply with these may mean that the cost of any actions the company takes without the insurer's approval will not be recoverable under the policy. They could also invalidate the policy in its entirety.

9.6   Dealing with the stock market (listed companies)

As we have already noted, where a company's shares are listed on an exchange and sizeable fraud is discovered – one of such a scale that it may make a significant impact on the company's finances – it may be necessary to make an announcement to the market, so as to avoid a false market in the company's shares being created.

In certain cases, shares may even need to be suspended, as the following case illustrates:

Betex suspended over Chinese fraud fears

Published: 19 April 2007

Shares in the AIM-listed lottery specialist Betex were suspended yesterday after two of its senior software staff were arrested and a third went on the run.

Betex, which became the first foreign investor in China's sports lottery, said two senior members of staff at its Beijing operation had been detained and the third was being sought by the Chinese police authorities in the province of Jilin.

"The company believes that the alleged illegal activity relates to conduct by these individuals and does not call into question the legality of the company's software product, or the conduct of the company," a spokesman said. It is thought the three were attempting to defraud Betex.

"Owing to the uncertainty surrounding the situation, and the significance of these operations to the financial performance of the company, Betex has requested a temporary suspension of trading in its shares on AIM pending clarification of the situation," the spokesman added.

Shares in Betex were 8 per cent down at 32.5p before the suspension, giving the company a market capitalisation of £44m.

Betex, which listed on AIM last March, focuses its activities in Asia but its chief executive and finance director are based in London. In addition to its involvement in the Chinese state lottery through deals with Hebei and Guizhou province, it recently acquired three licensed betting offices in the UK. Earlier this year, it invested £4.75m in launching scratchcards in China.

Source: http://news.independent.co.uk/business/news/article2461486.ece

---

If the board is in any doubt as to whether an announcement is merited, advice should be taken promptly (however, as we have already observed, panicky snap judgements and precipitate announcements can be as damaging and misleading to the market as a failure to properly disclose the company's concerns).

The Aftermath of a Fraud:
Reputational Issues

10.1 General

As a general rule, a company which has been the victim of a fraud will not be keen to publicise this fact. This could be because:

- Whilst the investigation is underway, it may want to avoid tipping off the suspected perpetrator(s) if they are not yet aware that the fraud has been discovered;
- It may be keen to avoid any public concern that its systems and controls are inadequate – and therefore that its management is incompetent;
- Where the company is a financial institution, it may want to prevent a "run" on its accounts by customers concerned that their money may not be safe with it; and
- Even where there is no suggestion that the company's procedures were wanting, it may be unwilling to be perceived as a victim.

However, sooner or later – human nature being what it is – the news of an issue is likely to be out, and it may be better for the company to issue an announcement based on the true facts, insofar as they are known, rather than allowing ill-informed rumours to propagate and perhaps to generate unwarranted anxiety.

In particular, once the investigation team begins interviewing witnesses, asking for client and personnel files and the like, the internal "jungle telegraph" will probably alert staff – and thence their friends, relatives and others – that an issue is afoot. This may lead to matters becoming public in the worst possible way.

The manner in which a company decides to announce that an investigation is underway matters, since it can play a key part in public perceptions and the ensuing reputational and other collateral damage that it suffers.

Consistency of message can be key:

- if the marketing department of the company takes a "reassuring" line, insisting that all is well, that the issue is very minor and that matters are under control;
- whilst the operational director takes the "responsible and trustworthy" line, going on record to state that the company is taking the matter very seriously and will, if appropriate take punitive action against the perpetrators – including suspensions and terminations of employment;

then the company itself may be viewed as, at best, incompetent (the left hand not knowing what the right hand is doing) and at worst, deceptive (trying to "spin" its way out of the bad news).

Where possible, reporting in an honest, but favourable way can reduce the risk of a negative reaction by customers, employees and institutional investors alike. For this reason, you should consider involving your PR or marketing department as soon as some public announcement is likely to be necessary. The message to employees should be consistent with that given to the market (for listed companies) and the wider world (for the benefit of customers, suppliers and counterparties).

10.2   Internal communications

Unless the investigation is being kept confidential so as to avoid tipping off the suspects, or indeed to try and entrap the perpetrator, you should inform staff of developments as soon as this is possible and adviseable.

You may need to involve not only your PR department, but also the company's legal advisers, to ensure that inappropriate detail is not given out. In addition, of course, you should take care to preserve legal privilege over any staff announcement if this is at all possible. You should not (as we will see in Chapter 11) assume that just because a document has been prepared by or for your legal advisers, it will be privileged – this may depend on:

- who prepared the document;
- in what capacity they did so;
- what the purpose of the document was; and
- the need to report to staff.

Probably the safest course of action is to ensure that any announcements to staff are made orally.

Where any written communication regarding the fraud is made to staff (perhaps because of their number, or wide dispersal) you should do all you can to ensure they do not divulge its contents to third parties.

You may deal with this by:

- explicit instructions to staff;
- marking the documents "strictly confidential" or "privileged" (although this will not, of itself, ensure that the document is privileged); and/or

- making it one of the company's terms and conditions of employment that disclosure of such documents is a disciplinary offence.

10.3 Questions to consider in the event of a fraud risk crisis

In terms of the issues which may reflect on the company's reputation in the aftermath of a crisis, you should consider the following:

- **Have we reported to every agency or authority to whom we have an obligation to report?** There may be legal requirements to report to the regulator in your industry, and a failure to do so will compound the reputational damage that the company suffers. In addition, prompt reporting is likely to assist the company if the regulator or law enforcement authorities are considering enforcement action or criminal sanctions. The key is reporting the right information in a timely manner. Over-reporting of concerns that prove unwarranted may damage the company's reputation as much, or more, than under-reporting. Irrelevant information can actually hamper management of an incident.
- **What can the company do about unfortunate press coverage? Can it prevent certain press coverage or claim damages later for statements that prove to be untrue?** A major fraud will, if it becomes public knowledge, inevitably generate considerable press comment – much of which may be critical of the company. In order to ensure that matters such as privilege are properly dealt with, you may have routed your announcements through the law department – however, whilst their involvement is critical, legal advisers may not be the most appropriate people to act as public spokesperson for the company; indeed if the company's lawyer is seen to be speaking for it, this may create greater concerns in the public's mind than if one of the company's "own" has the courage to step forward.
- **What rights of access, inspection and document removal do the enforcement and inspection bodies have? What will happen to these documents once they leave the company's control?** Many regulators and law enforcement agencies have extensive statutory powers to carry out inspections and seize documents. Generally, they will be required to keep these documents confidential – but there may in some cases be concerns that they could be disclosed, for example should the matter ever result in court action. This

could result in damaging information becoming public as part of the discovery process – including information which has little to do with the fraud at hand You should ensure that you have taken advice before blindly complying with requests for documents, including as to the basis on which the documents are being requested, and how they might be handled once out of your hands. You should also keep a record/copies of any documents disclosed to regulators in this way.

- **Customer detriment.** If customers have suffered some detriment (for example, because their accounts have been emptied by fraudsters, or because sensitive personal information about them has been stolen), is there some way in which the company can help them – and is the attendant publicity likely to be helpful (company supports its stakeholders in difficult times), or unhelpful? (perceived as an admission of liability?)
- **If disciplinary action is contemplated against an employee implicated in the fraud, should this be publicised?** This will depend upon the circumstances; in some cases an announcement of disciplinary action will only serve to escalate the public's concerns – matters are worse than they had feared! In others, it serves to give a positive message – the company is acting responsibly and taking the matter extremely seriously. Those responsible for the fraud – whether through dishonesty or incompetence – will not be left in charge of customer or shareholder assets any longer.
- **Are any regulatory sanctions likely to be public?** Many regulators, such as the FSA, have – and use – extensive powers to "name and shame" miscreants In such cases it may benefit the company to have the "bad news" out in the market before the regulatory announcement is made (provided to do so is not itself contrary to any regulations, etc, and will not prejudice any investigation).
- **Is there anything to be learned from other companies' experiences?** Often the PR and reputational impact of events can be gauged by looking at th experience of other organisations that have been the victim of similar frauds and how they responded.
- **Have newly created documents, including press releases, been reviewed from a legal perspective?** You should not allow any press releases or similar to be made without their having been reviewed by your legal adviser first – this includes statements of apology or regret for customer inconvenience. In addition you may find that if insurers are involved, they require an opportunity to approve any public statements. You should ensure that you

post-fraud action plan includes mechanisms to ensure that any legal/insurer approvals can be obtained without delay.

10.4 Public relations

If the company is listed or its shares are otherwise in public hands, and has either of regulatory (e.g. stock exchange) reporting requirements and/or high levels of outside interest in its affairs, you may need to pilot your way through some significant PR issues throughout the investigation process.

Such issues are not always obvious to non-PR professionals such as accountants, lawyers and the like: thus it is a good idea to involve your PR/corporate affairs department or advisers on the investigation team, from start to finish of the process.

Some Aspects of The Law
re Evidence, Privilege
and Fraud Investigation

11.1 Legal issues on an investigation

When a fraud investigation is instigated, one of the first steps you should consider taking is to involve the legal department. Their job will be to advise you not only on the conduct of the investigation itself, but also on various ancillary matters. Whether you involve external legal advisers will depend on a range of factors, including the complexity of the case, the availability of in-house legal resource and the size of the sums at issue.

Where legal advice is felt necessary, as a first step, you should meet with your advisers (whether in-house or external) and summarise the situation for them. You should ask your legal adviser (whether in-house or external) to advise you on the following:

- The structure of the investigation, and to give you some preliminary advice on matters such as privilege;
- The proper conduct of the investigation, and in particular any steps you should be taking with regard to the collection of evidence and interviewing of witnesses;
- Employment issues, especially where you are considering suspending or terminating someone's employment;
- Whether you should be making any reports to regulators and/or the law enforcement authorities;
- Whether you should be notifying the business' insurers of the potential or actual loss;
- The likelihood of any investigations by regulators and the police;
- Potential liabilities of the company and claims against third parties that the company may have.

We have touched on a number of these issues already when looking at the practical issues that arise when managing the aftermath of a fraud; in this chapter we will focus mainly on the law in respect of evidence and privilege, since this is one of the less practical but more complex areas.

1.2 The concept of privilege

The concept of "privilege" is important in countries such as the UK, where there is a system of document disclosure in force when matters go to court – and where damaging documents might therefore have to be shown to the opposite party in civil court actions unless they are categorised as privileged.

> *Legal privilege:* The principle that confidential communications between a lawyer and his client may not normally be disclosed without the client's consent.
>
> "Attorney-client privilege", or "legal professional privilege" as it is usually known in the UK, is a fundamental and substantive right, regarded as being an important constitutional safeguard for the rights of citizens – to the extent that in many cases it takes precedence over other public interest and policy considerations, in both civil and criminal cases.
>
> Without privilege, individuals could well be dissuaded from seeking the legal advice and representation to which they are properly entitled – resulting in much unwarranted damage. If you cannot disclose your true situation to your lawyer, in absolute confidence, how can you determine your true position and the correct course of action?

(This could be damaging not only because of their disclosure to the opposing party, but also because of their becoming public to the world at large).

This is therefore an area where you should consider taking legal advice, whether from in-house counsel or your external legal advisers.

11.3 Privilege and investigation reports

Certainly, if you or your legal advisers are preparing an internal investigation report, the following guidelines should be followed:

- An explanation of the meaning, implications and working of privilege in the UK (and in any other relevant jurisdictions) should be prepared and provided to *all those involved* with the investigation – to ensure that they all understand the importance of maintaining it wherever possible;
- Your colleagues should be advised that they should not prepare any new interim documents unless they will attract privilege – this is especially the case if they are critical of any aspects of the business, or if they would harm the company's case in any subsequent litigation;
- Depending on the rules of privilege for lawyers and accountants in the jurisdiction concerned, it is advisable to consider which of the following should prepare the report:

- lawyers (in-house or external);
- accountants;
- lawyers with the assistance of accountants.

- If privilege for a combined (lawyers/accountants) fact-finding report would be lost, you should consider organising the preparation of a separate accountants' report – or separating out the legal advice from the fact-finding element of the report;
- Any report should be structured so as to maximise the likelihood of privilege being preserved. For example, if it is possible, legitimate and appropriate, it may support your case if facts and legal advice are interwoven within the same document – so that they flow one from the other;
- For the avoidance of doubt as to your intention, the report should be marked "Privileged and Confidential". This will not, of itself, guarantee privileged status but may clarify that the document is intended to have the status of those to which privilege extends;
- You should ensure that:
  - You make only authorised, numbered, copies of the report;
  - A record is kept of their whereabouts, and to whom they have been released/loaned;
  - Those accessing the report are under instructions as to how to handle it; and
  - The copies can be recalled at any time.

1.4 Maintaining privilege

During a fraud investigation, you may have to consider privilege when:

- Dealing with the press;
- Corresponding with third parties connected with the recovery efforts (including law enforcement, regulators, insurers and witnesses);
- Keeping staff informed of progress.

As we have noted, each member of the fraud investigation team should be made aware of the privilege rules so as to preserve, insofar as is possible, the organisation's position should there be any subsequent litigation. Privilege belongs to the client (in this case, your organisation) and not to its lawyer – so the ability to waive privilege, whether intentionally or unintentionally, rests with the organisation.

Documents to which legal professional privilege attaches need not be disclosed in legal proceedings; this is why you should make every effort to maintain it – especially in the case of confidential material, or items of a commercially or reputationally sensitive nature (e.g. those critical of the company's conduct).

For clarity, the term "documents" includes:

- Paper documents;
- Computer tapes, discs and similar records;
- Sound and video recordings;
- Photographs and drawings;
- Plans;
- Microfiche and microfilm;
- Printouts from various recording devices.

They may attract privilege if they fall into any of the following categories:

- Correspondence between a client and its lawyers, whether or not in connection with litigation, which is confidential and written for the purpose of giving or obtaining legal advice (including correspondence with in-house lawyers, unless it relates to administrative matters and not legal advice). This is called legal advice privilege;
- The lawyers' file notes, drafts, instructions and briefs to counsel, and counsel's opinions and notes in connection with the above, whether or not connected with litigation;
- Correspondence between a client, its lawyers or its agent, and a third party prepared for the sole or main purpose of giving or getting legal advice or litigation – as well as experts' reports and witness statements prepared for similar reasons (unless and until they have been disclosed to the other side). This is called litigation privilege, and it might, for example, include correspondence with an investigatory or enquiry agent), and obviously exclude open correspondence with the opposing side's lawyers.

The following relevant categories of documents do *not* generally attract privilege

- Those drafted with a view to furthering an illegal act (such as, most pertinently, a fraud). The fact of whether the lawyer is aware of the fraud is irrelevant.
- Notes regarding the litigation (even those marked "privileged" or "confidential") prepared by the company for its own internal purposes, *unless* they are for:

- reporting *when strictly necessary* to others within the company on advice which has been received from lawyers; or
  - seeking information requested by lawyers.
- Board minutes recording discussion of the proceedings (unless these are for the purposes described above);
- Notes to the published accounts (and any provision) concerning the litigation, and/or any related correspondence with the company's accountants;
- Correspondence between the company and outside parties other than its own lawyers, or minutes/memoranda of such communications (including informal, handwritten notes) – unless these were drafted for the dominant purpose of obtaining legal advice in connection with existing or contemplated proceedings.

In particular, you should not assume that all documents created after litigation has commenced are automatically privileged – they are not. Thus, it is important that you stress to all concerned the need for great care and restraint when creating documents relating to proceedings.

Wherever possible, you should encourage your team to communicate orally or through lawyers with outsiders. Aside from the obvious concerns over aspects such as PR, your key concern should be to prevent disclosure to the fraudster himself of any legal advice on issues such as the strength of the underlying claims.

11.5   Case law: *Director of the Serious Fraud Office ex parte Smith*

Deals with SFO Investigations and an Individuals' Right to Silence

In the early 1990s (1992), a judgement from the House of Lords addressed the issue of judgment dealt with the question of whether a person being questioned by the Serious Fraud Office ("the SFO") has the right to silence.

The SFO is a government department. Its remit is to investigate and prosecute serious and complex frauds. These are defined as those where:

- the sum defrauded exceeds £1m; or
- there is an international aspect to the fraud (e.g. entities in several countries are involved); or

- specialised knowledge is needed to investigate it (for example of the finance system); or
- the case is likely to be of public interest and concern; or
- Where special powers are needed, which are reserved for the SFO and not available to other law enforcement agencies.

For more information, see www.sfo.gov.uk

The SFO derives its powers through powers delegated to its Director, under the Criminal Justice Act 1987 (CJA). These include, at Section 2 of that act, powers for the Director to require someone to:

- answer questions;
- provide information; or
- produce documents.

to assist the SFO in an investigation. The Director can investigate any suspected offence which, in his opinion, appears to include serious or complex fraud. Such notices are typically served not only on the fraudsters themselves, but on the business who may have knowingly or unknowingly been involved in the fraud – for example, banks, lawyers, accountants and the like.

Many of these businesses – and perhaps your own – owe a "duty of care and confidentiality" to their clients – whether statutory or otherwise, and so they are cautious about complying; however a Section 2 notice compels them to comply by law, so they can do so without fear of breaching these duties.

But what about the right of a person not to incriminate himself? There are limitations on whether information gained by the SFO under a Section 2 notice can be used against the giver.

Essentially, a statement made by someone in response to a such a requirement can only be used in evidence against him:

- In prosecuting him for having made a false statement in response to tha Section 2 notice (this an offence under Section 2(14) of the CJA 1987); or
- In prosecuting him for some other offence, where – in giving evidence – h makes a statement inconsistent with it (Section 2(8) of the same act).

It is also an offence for someone not to comply with a Section 2 request withou a "reasonable excuse" (*Section 2(13) of the CJA*).

The following case illustrates the fact that "reasonable excuse" cannot, however, be taken to extend to a wish (or the right) not to incriminate oneself.

Case study: *R v. Director of the Serious Fraud Office Ex Parte Smith* – House of Lords (11 June 1992) *The Times* 16 June 1992.

Facts. Mr Smith was the chairman and managing director of Wallace Smith Trust Co. Limited.

In April 1991, he told the Bank of England that the company was in financial difficulty. The police were called, and next day they arrested Mr Smith.

On 30th April, after several interviews, Mr Smith was charged with having been knowingly a party to the carrying on of the company's business with intent to defraud its creditors, contrary to Section 458 of the Companies Act 1985.

Having been charged, Mr Smith was cautioned, as required by Code C of the Police and Criminal Evidence Act 1984. He was subsequently granted bail.

While he was on bail the SFO issued a Section 2 notice, requiring that he attend its offices to answer questions and provide information. He applied to the Court for an order to say that he had no obligation to answer questions put pursuant to such a notice, once he had been charged. His grounds were:

- That the "natural sense" of the words of the Criminal Justice Act (i.e. the way in which an ordinary person would interpret them) meant that the SFO's power to require answers from someone ceased from the point at which they were charged; and
- That in any case, there was a conflict with Code C of the Police and Criminal Justice Act 1984, which *inter alia* established a "right of silence" – so that there was an implied exception to the Section 2 rules, for people who had been charged.

Decision. The Lords decided that the expression "right of silence" did not denote any single right, but rather a range immunities, of varying degrees of importance. In any event, they said that it is unrealistic to suggest that once someone has been charged, he is no longer someone whose affairs are under investigation in such a way that there can no longer be "any matter relevant to the investigation" (*Section 2(2) of the Act*).

Thus this first argument of Mr Smith's fell down.

On his second point, the Lords felt there a statute could only remove someone's right of silence if there were very good reasons – since the "privilege" against self-incrimination was *"deep rooted in English law"*. However, there were precedents, although the Criminal Justice Act 1987 did seem to go further than others.

So far as the Section 2 obligations conflicted with Code C in this wise, they said that the Code C protections were not directly linked to the privilege against self-incrimination. Rather they were there to ensure that someone condemning himself really did so of his own free will.

(This is why someone in custody, and therefore in a very vulnerable position, may not be questioned after a certain point – and why his answers to any such questioning are generally excluded from evidence.)

Having taken that on board, Mr Smith's second argument fell away. The Section 2 obligations were there to ensure he gave responses: it was of no matter that they were not voluntary – this was the whole point of the Section 2 powers.

Thus, both of Mr Smith's arguments were rejected.

11.6 Fraud investigations and the requirement to disclose

Requests in connection with third-party frauds, including those overseas

So far, we have focussed mainly on cases where you may be required (or protected from the requirement) to disclose as a result of a fraud at your own company. However, it is worth considering that you may be required to disclose documents in connection with frauds perpetrated on other parties.

One good illustration of this arose in the US with the collapse of Enron; the disclosure implications arising from this corporate fraud were not restricted the immediate perpetrators or victims, and had consequences for a number of UK businesses as well as those in the US and elsewhere.

The New York court handling Enron's bankruptcy issued subpoenas addressed to more than 40 law firms (including some in the UK). These sought the production of a range of documents related to Enron's bankruptcy.

The subpoenas were apparently quite wide-ranging, and included documents relating or belonging to other clients of the firms involved. They created considerable concern over possible breaches of confidentiality, with varied outcomes.

These are not new challenges; legal advisers, accountants, banks and other institutions do periodically find themselves inadvertently caught up in the fall out from large scale frauds, with possible implications for their clients and taxing questions as to the interaction of foreign information-gathering exercises with local duties of care, confidentiality and privilege. The UK courts regularly grapple with the inherent conflict between:

- A foreign court asserting extra-territorial jurisdiction; and
- the duty of the court of local jurisdiction to enforce obligations of confidentiality in accordance with local law.

These issues are often not easily resolved, and can result in lengthy and expensive satellite litigation (i.e. not related to the core matter under investigation) – for the eaglly, minded, an example would be *Pharaon and Others* v. *Bank of Credit and Commerce International SA (in liquidation) (Price Waterhouse (a firm) intervening) [1998] 4 All ER 455*. Again, if you find yourself subject to information requests from overseas, you should seek appropriately qualified legal advice.

Litigation

Excepting for the special, but limited, circumstances in which documents are protected by legal professional privilege (see above), the civil justice system in the UK requires that each of the opposing parties show his hand before the trial. This is mainly with a view to encouraging early settlement and equality of information.

So as to ensure that both sides adhere to this "cards on the table" regime, they are required to disclose to the opposing side all documents "relating to any matter in question between them in the action" – that is, any *relevant* document must be disclosed.

Of course, there is then the question of what is "relevant". The key test has for a long time been taken to be a case from the late 1800s, *Compagnie Financière du Pacifique* v. *Peruvian Guano Co. [1882]* (*11 QBD 55*): this standard has been re-confirmed in recent years, and the current standard of relevance, as cited more recently in *Thorpe* v. *Chief Constable of Greater Manchester [1989]* (*1 WLR 665*) is therefore taken to be as follows:

> *any document must be disclosed which it is reasonable to suppose contains information which may enable the other party either to advance his own case or to damage that of his adversary, or which may fairly lead him to a train of enquiry which may have either of these two consequences.*

The practical consequences of this are that:

- If you are involved in litigation, you may be required to disclose documents which may be damaging to your own case;
- The cost of complying with the discovery requirement is substantial in all but the smallest cases, involving management and employee time, the cost of legal advice, and expense in copying, organising and monitoring bundles of disclosed documents. It may in some cases even outweigh the amounts being litigated over.

To an extent, there is a risk that in any case some damaging or unhelpful documents will need to be disclosed. However, we can at least distinguish between:

- Unhelpful contemporaneous documentation (i.e. that created at the time of the original problem being litigated), about the existence of which not much can be done; and
- Documentation which is created after the problem arose, which as we have already seen can sometimes be managed or prevented.

This is why a system of proper document management should be a key element of your fraud investigation management process; it can help you to reduce the company's exposure to the risk of both existing and newly created documents.

Regulatory requirements

You may also be required to disclose documents to third parties if you are operating in a regulated industry, or involved in a fraud where others are regulated by bodies with far-reaching information gathering powers.

Such regulatory bodies are chiefly interested in furthering their own regulatory functions, and the complications visited on your business by such disclosures may not be high on their agendas.

Most businesses wish to comply with regulatory authorities, when those authorities are operating properly within their remits. However, the risks that can arise from compliance include:

- The fact that once you have disclosed information, the way in which it is handled or communicated onwards is no longer within your control; and
- In many cases, where you provide a regulator with a document (of whatever type – whether a fraud investigation report, or a copy of other routine correspondence), it is not protected by any public interest immunity and may therefore be discloseable to a third-party litigant.

A case from the mid-1990s illustrates how unhelpful this can be:

Case study: *Kaufmann & others v. Credit Lyonnais Bank* (*The Times*, 1 February 1995)

In this case, the courts were asked to consider whether a private and confidential report produced by Credit Lyonnais and provided to one of its regulators (the then Securities and Futures Authority ("SFA"), since replaced by the Financial Services Authority) was protected by public interest immunity.

The issue arose during the course of litigation. Credit Lyonnais disclosed the existence of the private report to the opposing side at the discovery stage of proceedings, but did not want to give them a copy of it. It therefore tried to avoid doing so, arguing that to do so would undermine the public interest immunity which attached to protect the report in the hands of SFA. That argument depended upon SFA convincing the court that confidential reports provided to it by its regulated members were protected by public interest immunity.

The court ruled that the reports disclosed to SFA in confidence were *not* protected by public interest immunity – and therefore, that copies of it which had been kept by Credit Lyonnais had to be disclosed to the opposing side.

The litigation was settled shortly following disclosure, but the case neatly shows that:

- No distinction will be made between documents disclosed voluntarily and those which are subject to an obligation of disclosure; and
- Typically, regulators are permitted by statute to share information with other regulatory authorities in the furtherance of their functions (these regulator-to-regulator disclosure powers are sometimes termed "regulatory gateways").

The following checklist may be helpful in determining how to proceed if asked for documents by a regulator:

Checklist – request for regulatory disclosure

If your organisation is asked to disclose documents to a regulatory body with appropriate authority over it, you may find that you have to make a decision as to whether to comply very quickly. Nonetheless, the answer is not always an automatic "yes" – it is not unknown for regulators to attempt fishing expeditions which exceed their legal remit, either deliberately or unwittingly, and if you comply needlessly and prejudice your customers' confidentiality, or put the business at risk, further problems could ensue. You should consider the following:

- *Authority.* Does the regulator have the necessary authority to request documents? If in doubt, ask which powers they are exercising in requesting this information, and – if an order or similar is needed, ask also to see this. Make sure, also, that all the documents you are being asked for actually fall within the ambit of this order/power.
- *Capacity.* Does the individual requesting the information on behalf of the regulator have the appropriate capacity? This may affect his entitlement to it and the use to which it may be put.
- *Confidentiality.* Do the documents requested contain confidential information? This may not be grounds to resist the disclosure of documents, if the information is private to the company itself (e.g. business plans). If the documents contain information belonging to a third party to whom a duty of confidence is owed, however (for example a bank to its customer)

then proper legal grounds for the disclosure should exist – for example, compulsion at law. There may be additional precautions to be taken in these circumstances.

- *Dawn raids.* If the request is made as part of a surprise regulatory visit (a "dawn raid") you should establish whether the regulatory team has complied with the relevant legal requirements – not all regulators have the power to enter and search your premises, and some which do will normally require a warrant.

- *Legal professional privilege.* Does legal professional privilege protect the documents you have been asked to provide? Many regulatory authorities have no power to compel disclosure of legally privileged information.

- *Privilege against self-incrimination.* If, by complying with the request for documentation, there is a risk that the information may be used against an individual in connection with criminal proceedings, consider whether or not the company is entitled to resist disclosure.

- *Procedural impropriety.* Is the request for documents oppressive? In 1996 Northern Bank successfully challenged 13 Notices issued by the Inland Revenue under the Taxes Management Act 1970 (*R v. O'Kane & Clarke – ex parte Northern Bank, The Times*, 10 October 1996) on the grounds that they were grossly oppressive, unfair and thus irrational. This is more likely to apply in circumstances where the documentation requested is in connection with a third party, than where they relate to your business itself.

11.7 What types of document should you be most concerned about?

As we have noted, the documents which might have to be disclosed when litigating fraud, or when under an obligation to make a regulatory report on the matter, fall broadly into two camps:

1. Contemporaneous documents and source material – those documents created in the ordinary course of business – perhaps at or around the time of the fraud, but in any event not related to its investigation or litigation. These are already in existence, and not much can be done about them; they will, if not already destroyed as part of a routine document management policy, most likely have to be disclosed in any event. They will include accounting

records, customer/client records, notes, correspondence, memoranda, board minutes and emails.

2. Documents which are produced specifically in relation to the issue at hand – whether it be the investigation of the potential fraud, or its prosecution, or the company's potential exposure to the problem, assessment of weaknesses in systems and controls which permitted the fraud to be perpetrated, or notification to insurers. They will include:

   - formal items such as board or risk audit minutes; and
   - reports to the regulators, and informal items – notably emails and the like.

We will look at some issues relating to both categories – contemporaneous and new documents – and round up with how you might, with an eye to the future, want to review your company's document retention policy to minimise risk in the event of future problems.

Contemporaneous documents

As we have already said, there is not much that can be done about these – and if they are still in existence, you will probably have to disclose them if a matter comes to litigation. The most damaging can be those documents which are relatively informal, since these are invariably created in haste and without great thought:

- *Emails* suffer from these characteristics more than many other types of document, since they are often thought of as being simply an online "conversation" – with all the casualness that individuals employ when chatting informally by the water cooler. Email is undoubtedly a blessing in many ways; it allows for speed, it is simple and it can be secure. It is nonetheless a *mixed* blessing, as is shown by the many well-worn cases where companies and individuals have been found guilty on the production of some unfortunate email correspondence. In addition, the increasing quantity of email communication has most definitely impinged on general quality:
  - Because they are so quick to draft and send, emails are often ill-considered (or not considered at all), "off the cuff" and far more informal than even intra-office memoranda;
  - They often lack the benefit of being placed in context. An unfortunate email message, read out of the context in which it was drafted, can be fa

more damaging than one seen in the light of the surrounding correspondence or circumstances;

- Individuals may believe that because they draft their own emails direct to their own PC (instead of sending a letter down to the secretary to be typed, or having a bank instruction reviewed by a supervisor), it is in some way "private". In the context of discovery, this will not be the case at all.
- Depending on a company's system of IT back-ups, an email may have a much longer life than hard-copy documents. This is because even if sender and recipient delete the message, all they usually achieve is the deletion of the message index from their in/sent boxes and not the sending of the message itself on the corporate system. The message will still be retrievable on the individual's (and the recipient's) hard disk and may be recoverable even if it is overwritten.

- *Other records on employee PCs.* These may include faxes sent direct from PCs, and the fact that this can be done straight from the desktop (rather than via hard copy) may mean that there is less supervisory oversight, or thought, than would otherwise be the case.
- *Private notes, diary entries and memoranda.* These can be even more informal than emails because of the shorthand way in which they are often created (handwritten, often in haste, perhaps initially intended only as a temporary *aide memoire* destined for the bin – but ending up retained indefinitely). Unlike documents such as board minutes, which are usually prepared with a measure of care, private notes may be something as simple as a scribbled reminder or observation. Given the way these notes may be drafted and/or copied, it can also be difficult to keep track of their whereabouts.

There are various practical steps you can, as a risk manager, take to minimise the opportunity for disaster if and when a suspected fraud, or other event calling for potential disclosures, occurs. These include:

Training

Make your colleagues and staff aware of the risk the above documents can present, and encourage a responsible communication culture in the business. A programme of training and set of written guidelines, supported by regular reinforcement messages, should convey the message that all documented types of communication – whether formal or informal, written or pictorial, electronic or hard copy, are liable to be seen by outsiders.

New documents

If and when a potential fraud is identified, (or indeed some other problem), take prompt control so as to minimise the scope for confusion and the creation of additional problems. In severe cases you may wish to notify a wide number of staff, possibly on a cascade basis similar to that used for disaster planning – so as to solicit internal reports from a variety of specific divisions, with a view to establishing how best to proceed. You will probably be doing this before either:

- Litigation is underway or decided upon; or
- The regulator has been informed, if this is a requirement of your particular industry.

This can be a key risk point – in particular there is the danger that such documents (and this may include formal board minutes as well as executive summaries) may record discussions of the merits of a company's position which will not be legally privileged and which will be available for all to see.

The same may also be true of memoranda or reports which are prepared by departments which have to report on "problem" issues, such as compliance, special projects or operations and credit risk or credit control.

Risks arise in these areas because these departments are often charged with preparing briefings or reports, whether for internal or parent company purposes or regulators (see "Newly created external reports" below), which are designed to inform senior managers or the board of potential problems, and to give them adequate information on which to base remedial action.

It is easy to envisage such difficulties if, for example, a life insurance company falls victim to a fraud, disgruntled policyholders sue it for negligence and discovery reveals a raft of internal reports and memoranda detailing who knew what, and when, and setting out in gory detail all the perceived deficiencies in the company's internal systems. The apportionment of blame between different departments can exacerbate the situation: the documents may have been drafted under the influence of two perfectly natural human characteristics – eagerness to be helpful, and concern to protect one's back. Unfortunately, this will often give rise to an extremely full, warts-and-all account supplemented by supposition as to how the situation arose and who was responsible for it. In a sense, such reports are accusatory and confessional in nature.

Such documents can be highly damaging, and whilst on the face of it they fulfil particular need – to inform management and the board of the facts – you shoul consider, before they are instigated, what form they should take and whether they are actually necessary at all.

External reports

Some similar comments can apply to reports prepared for insurers, law enforcement authorities or regulators. It is not unusual for a business to commission a report on the facts, in order to demonstrate its commitment to establishing what has gone wrong, and to preventing its recurrence. Whilst the intentions behind this are laudable, again you should consider carefully the form of, and need for, such a report.

Legal professional privilege

As we have already read, privilege is a rule which can give a legal adviser's client the right to withhold documents from discovery to a court, or similar body, and thereby avoid potentially damaging or embarrassing disclosures. In theory, as we have also seen in the Kaufmann case above, it does not protect from disclosure documents requested by regulatory authorities. However, its effect has been extended to limit the entitlement of *some* regulatory authorities to compel disclosure of legally privileged documents; you should establish the situation with regard to your own regulator before responding to requests for documents.

With some exceptions, legal advice provided by your company's in-house lawyer will benefit from privilege in the same way as advice from an external lawyer. This will not, however, be the case if (for example) the correspondence relates to work an in-house lawyer is undertaking on a non-legal task – or which a legally-qualified individual is doing in a non-legal capacity, such as acting as compliance officer, or carrying out essentially executive or managerial functions.

Checklist: The creation of new documents on discovery of a potential fraud

- Ask yourself whether it is really essential to create this document – many matters can be adequately dealt with orally.
- Written reports should consist of neutral statements of fact, not opinion or conjecture. Concise records of actions in particularly sensitive matters may be potentially valuable records for the future. They can still,

however, be helpful to an opponent in this context, not least because you will have prepared them with the benefit of access to larger numbers of people within the organisation than the opposing party will have in any litigation (that is, you have full and easy access to your employees and records: the other side does not).

- If documents must record opinions – which may be necessary – they should include the rationale, so as to minimise their being misconstrued or misrepresented by some hostile third party with the benefit of hindsight.
- Who really needs a copy of the document? The list may be shorter than you think – and if the recipients feel compelled to express their views in response, these may be unhelpfully worded.
- Some companies have a rule that meeting notes are not taken away from meetings by attendees, so that only a central minute is retained for general record-keeping purposes.
- Consider the benefits of a proper document retention, and destruction, policy expending not only to paper documents, but also to voice recordings, emails and electronic records (for document retention policies, see later).
- Discourage employees from retaining so called "private files", diaries and notebooks.

11.8 Document management to preserve privilege

Proper document management will from time to time include corresponding with your in-house legal department, or external lawyers, to ensure that legal professional privilege can legitimately be asserted. Although it is not practical or legitimate to route all communication through lawyers for this purpose, there are – as we have already noted – situations where privilege is available, and may be legitimately asserted, and which are often under-used due to lack of understanding and/or planning.

For example, if – given the foregoing discussions of internal and external fraud investigation – you decide that such a document is required, then to the extent that this can be made subject to legal professional privilege, it will be kept out of the discovery arena and its contents will remain privy only to those within the company. So a document which is prepared primarily as a brief for lawyers, is order to seek their advice on the company's legal position, rather than for more general consumption – even if sight of it may be given to others at a later stage and in controlled circumstances – may be privileged.

In the preparation of such a report, you should if possible manage the information-gathering process so that the company can claim privilege over any additional or supporting non-contemporaneous material too. The aim is to ensure that the only documents liable to discovery, or to a request for disclosure from regulators, are those representing direct evidence of the events.

The way in which you manage this process is important: as well as achieving the aim of privilege for as many documents as possible, you should, ideally, increase your colleagues' general awareness of risks associated with document creation.

When a problem does arise, you should as a first step towards securing privilege, consider instructing your in-house or external lawyer to do the following:

- Provide the company with legal advice on the problem; and
- Gather, from within the company, all available documents and information which may have any bearing on the problem, also for the purpose of giving legal advice.

This should mean that any newly created document will have been produced for the purpose of giving/receiving legal advice, and will be privileged. This may enable your company to use the resulting material for a frank and full analysis of the situation, and the risks to which it has been exposed.

The material distinction between legal advice privilege and litigation privilege is as follows: if the information compiled to enable the lawyer to give advice includes material from an external source, it will only be privileged if litigation privilege applies.

1.9   Document retention

Of course, a damaging document can only be disclosed if it still exists – but no sensible company would embark on a process of document destruction knowing that litigation or other disclosure requirements are imminent: to do so could mean that the company, and potentially also its personnel, fall foul of various laws – not to mention the inferences which could be drawn from a sudden spate of shredding just as litigation looms on the horizon! However, a good document management system allows a business to destroy, on a routine basis, those documents which it no longer needs, enabling it to:

- save storage space and reduce fire risks;
- avoid falling foul of the Data Protection Act 1998;
- make it easier to locate current documents, and those older documents which must – for whatever reason – be retained; and
- finally, as a "collateral benefit", avoid the unhelpful disclosure of aged documents which may weaken the company's position.

Such a policy will only have value, however, if it is credible and of reasonably long standing: again, negative inferences will be drawn if a document retention (or document destruction) policy is implemented immediately on the identification of problems. It will carry much greater weight and credibility if it has been in place for some time, and has been applied consistently.

There is no single set of rules for a sound document management policy – this will depend on the nature and scale of the business, and the risks and laws to which it is subject. However the following checklist may prove of value:

Checklist: Document retention policy

External factors. Any statutory or regulatory requirements to retain certain classes of business records for a specified minimum period (for example, regulated financial services businesses should retain reports of anti-money laundering suspicions referred to the law enforcement authorities indefinitely); similarly, the Companies Acts place certain retention requirements on companies in connection with their accounting records. Your policies should identify which documents are subject to such requirements.

Internal factors.

- Consider which departments or people are most likely to receive or generate documents, what type of documents these are, and what risks may be associated with them. Generally speaking, those which record opinion or evaluate performance have the greatest potential to do damage. This means that departments such as Internal Audit, or Compliance, may run a higher risk than others.

- Establish appropriate guidelines on retention for each type of document, identifying which ones are to be retained and for how long. This is a sizeable task, and the schedule will need reviewing periodically as new types of document are created.

Retention/destruction. From the above, determine which documents can legitimately be destroyed, and how long others should be retained. Consider:

- When might each type of document be required in future?
- What will happen if they are not available?
- For example, litigants are expected to retain contemporaneous documents which evidence a transaction or which provide a first hand record of events, and it reflects badly if these are destroyed in haste. However compromising, they should be retained for as long as possible and at least for any relevant limitation period. For example, consider retaining for at least six years from the date of creation contemporaneous documents which evidence the performance of contractual obligations.

Consistency. The policy must be consistent. Do not have different rules for similar classes of documents without justification.

Review. Review the policy regularly, and if need be update it for new document types or new legislation/regulations.

Scanning. If the volume of documentation to be retained is substantial, it may ultimately be more cost effective for documents to be electronically scanned and recorded on to a computer. This will both save space, and lend itself to flexible and helpful cataloguing. The process of scanning and electronic storage should itself be properly documented to avoid any future suggestion that documents may have been tampered with.

1.10 Law regathering evidence

Case Law: *St Merryn Meat Ltd & Others v. Hawkins & Others [2001]*

Deals with: *Acceptable Methods of Gathering Evidence*

In 2001, a case was heard which provided an excellent example of the potential pitfalls of using improper methods to obtain evidence.

155

The aim of the evidence gathering was to support an application for a freezing order, and the case showed that such improper methods could ultimately result in the order's being discharged – regardless of the merits of the claimant's case against the defendant.

The facts: In *St Merryn's*, evidence of the defendants' alleged fraud was obtained by bugging home telephones.

In applying to discharge the freezing orders that had been obtained, the defendants alleged material non-disclosure by the claimants and argued that their conduct was itself a criminal offence under the Interception of Communications Act 1995.

They further alleged that it was a breach of Article 8 of the European Convention on Human Rights (ECHR). Article 8(1) of the ECHR (now incorporated into the Human Rights Act 1998) provides that: "Everyone has the right to respect for his private and family life, his home and his correspondence."

The judge stated: "It is relatively well established that the court should modify any remedies it grants so as to comply with Convention rights [*meaning, here, the ECHR*] . . . It seems to me that the court considering an interim application would have wanted to be satisfied that any order it made did not involve a breach of Article 8 . . . Here it is suggested that, because the evidence for the application had been obtained by a method which infringed Article 8(1) [*i.e. the right to respect for private correspondence*], the court should have been informed [*in deciding whether to grant the freezing order*]. I have formed the view that the method of obtaining this evidence was relevant to the court's decision with or without overt unlawfulness. The fact that a right under Article 8 had been violated made this disclosure all the more important."

So, even though the defendants in the action admitted their involvement in fraudulent behaviour during the course of the application to set aside the freezing orders, the judge decided that their rights had been violated by the interception of their home telephone calls, and that this justified the discharge of the without-notice interim freezing orders that had previously been granted.

The case serves to illustrate the importance of obtaining evidence only in the proper way (and, when seeking freezing orders, of giving the courts all relevant information on how your evidence was obtained); again you may need to take advice.

Index

Abuse of position, fraud by, 6
Accounting-related frauds, 29
    warning signs, 58–9
Action plan, in fraud risk management, 45–6
Acts, of dishonesty and deception, 5
Advance fee fraud, 31–2
Aftermath, of a fraud
    comunicating the case
        to general, 127–8
        internal, 128–9
    issues reflecting reputation, 129–31
    public relations, 131
Agip (Africa) Limited v. Jackson & Ors, 22
Analytical method, in fraud risk management
    action plan, 45–6
    assessment of risk factors, 43–4
    cultural issues, 48–9
    identifying fraud indicators, 46–7
    identifying risk factors, 41–2
    involving management team, 44
    planning, 39
    statistical tools, 48
    understanding business processes, 39–41
Anti-competitive issues, 14
Anti-fraud measures, 11–12
Assets recovery agency (ARA), 14, 16
Assisting, in a fraudulent scheme, 20–1, 61–3
Attorney-client privilege, 136

Bank of Credit and Commerce International
    (BCCI), case study, 16–17
Barlow Clowes International Ltd
    (In Liquidation), case study, 20–1
Betex, case analysis, 124
Bid-rigging, 14
Bingham Report, 17
Bladon v. ALM Medical Services, case analysis,
    18–19
BNP Paribas Private Bank (BNPP Private Bank),
    case study, 119–20

Cartel-oriented issues, 14
Case laws, 139–42, 155–7
    on assisting in a fraud, 20–1
    on constructive knowledge, 21–2
Categories, in fraud
    examples of fraud events
        advance fee fraud, 31–2
        cheque frauds, 33–4
        corruption, 30
        fraudulent accounting, 29
        identity theft, 30–1
        insurance fraud, 31

        prime bank frauds, 32–3
        purchasing activity, 29
        theft, 29
    factors influencing fraud, 34–6
    general discussion, 27–9
Cheque and payment card fraud, 69
Cheque frauds, 33–4
CIFAS (the Credit Industry Fraud Advisory
    Service), 35, 69
Collusion, 7
Company's bankers and fraud event, 122–3
Company's insurers and fraud event, 123
Competition Act 1998, 14
Computer-related fraud, 10–11
Conspiracy to defraud, 5
Constructive knowledge, of fraudulent
    activity, 21–2
Corruption, 30
Credit card fraud, 68–9
Criminal Justice Act 1987, 19–20
Criminal offences, 7
Cultural issues, in fraud risk management, 44
Customer frauds, 68–70

Deception, 7–8
Defrauded business' insurers, 9
Disclosure, of investigation, 142–7
Dishonesty/intent, 8
Document handling, fraud management, 93–5
    contemporaneous documents and source
        material, 147–9
    external reports, 151
    fresh documents, creation of, 150–2
    legal advice documents, 151
    management strategy, 152–3
    retention policy, 153–5
    training and set of written guidelines, 149
Drug Trafficking Act 1994, 15

Eagle Trust Plc v. SBC Securities Limited, 22
Electronic banking frauds, 60–1
Embezzlement, 70
Employees, role in fraud, 10–12
Enterprise Act 2002, 14
Evidence handling, in fraud events
    gathering of evidences, case laws, 155–7
    preserving of evidence, 95
    sources of evidence, 93
External frauds
    categories
        customer, 68–70
        embezzlement, 70
        investment, 70–2

supplier, 67–8
   third party-against-customer fraud, 72–3
general discussion, 67
recovery steps, 73–4

Failing to disclose information, fraud by, 6
False representation, fraud by, 6
Financial Services Authority, of UK, 11
Forgery, 7
Fraud Act 2006, 6, 13–14
Fraud risk triangle, 41–2, 55–6
Fraud suspicion report log, 90

GAIN (the Gone Away Information Network),
   35, 69
Goods shipping frauds, 61

High profile frauds, 12
HR frauds, 59–60

Identity theft, 30–1
Immediate action, to crisis
   handling of communications, 97–8
   initial steps, 91
   legal issues, 98–9
   preserving, tracing and recovering lost assets,
     99–100
   on receipt of a fraud suspicion report, 89–90
   securing and preserving evidence, 91–5
Indicators, in fraud risk management, 46–7
Insurance fraud, 31
Internal frauds
   types
     accounting, 58–9
     assisting/colluding with external
       fraudsters, 61–3
     electronic banking fraud, 60–1
     goods shipping fraud, 61
     HR frauds, 59–60
     purchasing, 57–8
   vulnerability to, 55–6
Investigation team, 95–7
Investigation techniques and steps
   checklist, 107–8
   directors' duties and solvency, 109–10
   legal issues, 106–7
   option for employee representation, 105–6
   post-investigation review, 107–8
   recovery of funds, 111–13
   remedial steps, 109
   securing company assets, 108–9
   steps for conducting interviews, 104–5
   witness interrogation, 103

Investment frauds, 70–2
IT-related fraud, plans for non-IT professional
   assessment of IT environment, 77–8
   evaluation
     of historic records, 82–3
     of images taken, 81–2
   evidence collection, 80–1
   monitoring of activities, 83
   securing and preserving the technology, 78–9

Legal definition and laws, of fraud
   elements of, 7–8
   estimates and trends, 8–10
     government reactions, 12
     number of cases, 8–10
     persons involved, 10–12
   general discussion, 5–7
   laws
     case laws, 20–3
     Criminal Justice Act 1987, 19–20
     Enterprise Act 2002, 14
     Fraud Act 2006, 13–14
     overseas, 23
     Proceeds of Crime Act 2002, 14–16
     Public Interest Disclosure Act 1988
       (PIDA), 16–19
   non-statutory codes and guidance on risk
     management, 24
Legal issues, in investigation of fraud, 98–9, 135
   company's bankers, 122–3
   company's insurers, 123
   police and other enforcement authorities,
     121–2
   regulators, 117–21
   stock market, 123–4
Legal privilege, 136
Limitation of production fraud, 14

Management team, role in fraud risk
   management, 44
Market-sharing fraud, 14
Misappropriation, 7
Misreprensentation, 7
Money laundering offence, 15
Money Laundering Regulations 1993, 15

Non-statutory codes and guidance, on fraud risk
   management, 24

Phishing scams, 7
Planned approach, in fraud risk
   management, 39

Police and other enforcement authorities, in
    investigation of fraud, 121–2
Price-fixing fraud, 14
Prime bank frauds, 32–3
Prison sentence, 14
Privilege
    concept of, 135–6
    and investigation reports, 136–7
    maintaning of, 137–9
Proceeds of Crime Act 2002, 14–16
"Protected Disclosure" provisions, 18
Public Interest Disclosure Act 1988 (PIDA),
    16–19
Purchasing frauds, 29, 57–8

Recovery rates, 9
Refund fraud, 68
Regulators, in investigation of fraud, 117–21
Risk factors, of fraud, 41–2

Salami frauds, see Purchasing activity frauds
Salvation Army and a fraudulent investment
    opportunity, case analysis, 71

Sarbanes-Oxley Act, of the United States
    ("SOX"), 23
Serious and Organised Crime Authority
    (SOCA), 122
Specialist investment instruments, 70
Staff, role in fraud, see Employees, role in fraud
Stand-by letters of credit, 71
21st-century frauds, 5
Stock markets and fraud activity, 123–4
Supplier frauds, 67–8
Suspicious transaction report, 15

Theft, 7, 29
Theft Act 1968, 13
Thefts Acts 1968–96, 5
Third party-against-customer frauds, 72–3
Tracing lost assets, 100
Turnbull Committee Report, on internal
    controls, 24

Volumes, of fraud, 8

Printed and bound by CPI Group (UK) Ltd, Croydon, CR0 4YY

08/05/2025

01864859-0004